RED FOLEY'S

Cartoon History of Baseball

LITTLE SIMON
Simon & Schuster Building
Rockefeller Center,
1230 Avenue of the Americas,
New York, New York 10020
Text copyright ©1992 by MBKA.
Illustrations copyright ©1992 by S. B. Whitehead.
All rights reserved including the right of
reproduction in whole or in part in any form.
LITTLE SIMON is a trademark of Simon & Schuster.
Manufactured in Hong Kong.
10 9 8 7 6 5 4 3 2 1
ISBN 0-671-73627-2

**An
MBKA
Production**

RED FOLEY'S

Cartoon History of Baseball

ILLUSTRATED BY S.B. WHITEHEAD

Little Simon
Published by Simon & Schuster
New York London Toronto Sydney Tokyo Singapore

Baltimore Orioles

1955 — Future Hall of Fame third baseman Brooks Robinson debuts with Orioles. He is one of 54 players that manager–general manager Paul Richards employs during season, with club again finishing seventh.

PUT ME IN, COACH, I'M READY TO PLAY!

1953 — WE'VE FINALLY EARNED OUR WINGS!

The American League transfers St. Louis Browns' franchise to Baltimore in October. Club is refinanced and re-named "Orioles," after famous National League club of the 1890s.

1954 — HALP! I FORGOT IF I'M AN ORIOLE OR A YANKEE!

Following Orioles' seventh-place finish, Yankees and Birds execute largest player swap in history—a 17-man deal in which Baltimore receives 11 players.

1958

Veteran knuckleballer Hoyt Wilhelm no-hits the Yankees on September 20th at Baltimore. This is the club's first perfecto, as Orioles reach sixth place.

1963 — THIS BIRD IS THE WORD!

Left-hander Steve Barber becomes Orioles' first 20-game winner—a feat Birds' hurlers will perform 24 times in the next 21 seasons.

1965 — BALTIMORE? WHAT CAN I DO IN BALTIMORE?

Outfielder Frank Robinson is obtained from Cincinnati in December deal for three players. The trade is considered one of the most one-sided swaps of all time, with Robinson eventually reaching the Hall of Fame.

1966 — WORLD CHAMPS — BAUER POWER!

Orioles take American League flag. They wipe out Los Angeles Dodgers in four straight in World Series under manager Hank Bauer. Frank Robinson wins Triple Crown and MVP award.

Earl Weaver, who never reached majors as second baseman, is named Orioles' skipper in July. In the next 15 seasons his clubs will win one World Series, four pennants, and six Eastern Division titles.

With lefties Mike Cuellar and Dave McNally winning 23 and 20, respectively, Orioles capture American League East by 19 games but are upset by New York Mets in five-game World Series.

Cuellar, Palmer, and Pat Dobson each win 20; McNally wins 21. Orioles win third straight pennant but lose World Series in seven games to underdog Pirates.

Palmer wins 20 or more games for fourth straight season, but Orioles fail to reach World Series because they are defeated by Oakland A's in a five-game American League Championship Series.

Cuellar, veteran screwball pitcher, wins 22. Orioles again bow to Oakland in best-of-five pennant playoff, losing four in a row after Cuellar wins opener.

Reggie Jackson is acquired from Oakland. He plays only this season for Baltimore before opting for free agency. Birds finish second to Yankees in American League East.

BOOOOOOOG!!!

First baseman Boog Powell is American League's MVP. Cuellar, McNally, and Jim Palmer reach 20-win circle. Orioles win flag and defeat Cincinnati in five-game World Series.

1983

Shortstop Cal Ripken, Jr., American League's Rookie of the Year in '82, is league's MVP. Orioles, with Joe Altobelli as manager, defeat Philadelphia in five-game World Series.

THAT RIPKEN'S GOT ONE HECK OF A *RIP!*

1977

Eddie Murray, who is to star for Orioles for next decade, is named American League Rookie of the Year. Birds tie with Boston, 2½ games behind Yankees in hotly contested Eastern Division scramble.

1978

CAN WE JUST PLAY WITHOUT A THIRD BASEMAN?

Palmer wins at least 20 for eighth, and final, time in his career. Orioles sag to fourth place in American League East. It's the first season in 23 years that Brooks Robinson doesn't appear in Birds' lineup.

1979

TIME TO WALK THE PLANK AGAIN, BUCKO!

Lefty Mike Flanagan wins 23. Orioles lose seven-game World Series to Pittsburgh despite 102 regular-season wins and eight-game bulge over runner-up Milwaukee Brewers.

1980

SOLID AS A ROCK!

25

Right-hander Steve Stone, who never won more than 15 games while pitching for three other clubs prior to arrival in Baltimore, wins 25. He is named Cy Young Award recipient.

1981

STANDINGS

1ST HALF	2ND HALF
1. NEW	1. NEW
2. BALTIMORE	2.

2ND OR 4TH, ALL I KNOW IS THAT WE DIDN'T FINISH 1ST !!!

Right-hander Dennis Martinez is among league leaders with 14 victories in strike-interrupted season. Orioles finish second and fourth in split-season play.

1982

THAT'S IT! I'M GOIN' BACK TO THE FARM!

Earl Weaver retires as manager. Orioles finish second, one game behind Milwaukee in American League East race, which Birds could have knotted with win on season's final day.

Right-hander Mike Boddicker wins 20 and leads American League with 2.79 ERA, but Orioles slide to fifth, finishing 19 games behind Detroit, which goes on to win World Series.

Altobelli is fired as manager in mid-June and is replaced by Weaver. Orioles fail to respond to change and wind up in fourth place.

Orioles' seventh-place finish causes Weaver to retire once more. In post-season announcement, longtime third-base coach Cal Ripken, Sr., is named as replacement.

Ripken Sr., father of the shortstop, Cal Jr., and the second baseman, Billy, is unable to make Orioles contenders. They go 67–95 and finish sixth in American League East.

After Ripken's club opens 0–6, he is replaced by Frank Robinson as manager. But change has little effect, as Birds lose 107 and are anchored in American League East basement.

Cal Ripken, Jr., who has played in more consecutive games than any active player (1,411), sets fielding mark for errorless play by shortstop during season. Retired Jim Palmer is inducted into Hall of Fame.

Robinson does remarkable managing job, which earns him Manager of the Year honors. He leads Orioles to second-place finish. Club goes 87–75 and draws team-record 2.5 million at home.

Boston Red Sox

1914 Sox finish second, but in July Boston purchases 19-year-old Babe Ruth from Baltimore. In subsequent seasons he'll lead AL in pitching—and majors in home runs when he becomes an outfielder.

1901 PLEASE! WATCH THY LANGUAGE!

Boston is granted American League franchise, and club, known as the Pilgrims, or Puritans, finishes second under manager Jimmy Colins, a Hall of Fame third baseman. Right-hander Cy Young, 34, veteran of 11 NL seasons, leads team with 33 victories.

1903 ... SITTIN' ON TOP OF THE WORLD!

Club wins AL flag by 14½ games and defeats Pittsburgh in first World Series, five games to three, in best-of-nine showdown. Young leads AL with 28 wins, while Bill Dinneen, who wins three World Series games, chalks up 21 and Tom Hughes 20. Buck Freeman leads AL with 13 home runs.

1904 CHICKEN!

Boston wins pennant by 1½ games over New York on final day of season but goes no further, as New York Giants decline to meet them in World Series. Young wins 26, Dinneen 23, and veteran lefty Jess Tannehill 21, as Colins skippers team to its second AL flag.

1912 STAHL, LET'S PLAY BALL!

Fenway Park opens, and club, now known as the Red Sox, wins pennant by 14 games and seven-game World Series from New York Giants. Manager Jake Stahl's squad, with club-record 105 victories, is paced by Tris Speaker's .383 batting average, plus 34 wins (16 in a row) by righty Smoky Joe Wood.

1915 THIS SPEAKER LETS HIS BAT DO THE TALKING!

Under manager Bill Carrigan, Sox win flag and World Series in five games over Phillies. Speaker, in his final Boston season, bats .322. Right-handers Rube Foster and Ernie Shore lead staff with 19 wins each, while Ruth wins 18.

1916 CARRIGAN WIN AGAIN!

Carrigan's Sox again win pennant and five-game World Series over Brooklyn. Ruth wins 23 and his 1.75 ERA tops American League. Lefty Dutch Leonard and righty Carl Mays each register 18 victories.

Manager Ed Barrow guides Boston to AL flag and World Series win over Chicago Cubs in six games. Ruth, a part-time pitcher and part-time outfielder, wins 13 and leads AL with 11 homers. Mays heads staff with 21 victories.

Owner Harry Frazee sells Ruth to Yankees in January, and Sox sink to fifth place. It'll be 14 years before they return to the first division. Club finishes last in nine of the next 15 seasons after Frazee sells off his star players.

Williams leads league with .406 and 37 homers, but Sox finish second to New York. Cronin bats .311, but pitching doesn't match the offense. Dick Newsome is top winner with 19. Grove, in final year, wins seven, the last his 300th lifetime victory.

A year after Tom Yawkey purchases Red Sox, he begins buying players. After a fourth-place finish in 1934, he purchases Joe Cronin from Washington for Lyn Lary and $225,000 and makes him Boston's manager.

Red Sox introduce outfielder Ted Williams, who bats .327 and hits 31 homers while leading AL with 145 RBIs. First baseman Jimmie Foxx hits .360 and leads AL with 35 homers. Lefty Grove wins 15 games and paces AL with 2.54 ERA.

Red Sox win first postwar season flag by 12 games. Williams leads club with .342 average, plus 38 homers and 123 RBIs. Righty Dave Ferriss goes 25–6, and Tex Hughson wins 20. Sox, however, lose seven-game World Series to St. Louis.

Joe McCarthy, famed Yankees' manager, skippers Boston to second place when Cleveland defeats Sox in one-game playoff. Williams leads league with .369 average, and Vern Stephens paces club with 29 homers and 137 RBIs.

1967

Dick Williams becomes skipper and brings club from ninth to AL pennant by one game over Detroit and Minnesota. Righty Jim Lonborg wins 22, while outfielder Carl Yastrzemski wins Triple Crown with .326 average, 44 homers, and 121 RBIs. Boston's "Impossible Dream" vanishes when Sox bow to St. Louis in seven-game World Series.

YAZ! MVP!

1949

ALL'S MEL THAT ENDS WELL!

Despite lefty Mel Parnell's league-leading 25 wins and 2.77 ERA, Sox finish second, one game behind New York. Williams leads club with .343 average and AL with 43 homers. He and Stephens share RBI title with 159 apiece. Righty Ellis Kinder goes 23–6.

1975

DARN! WE WERE SO CLOSE!

WORLD CHAMPS

Sox, under Darrell Johnson, win AL East and down A's in pennant playoff. Rookie of the Year and MVP outfielder Fred Lynn hits .331, plus 21 homers and 105 RBIs. Outfielder Jim Rice bats .309 with 22 homers and 102 RBIs. Sox lose seven-game World Series to Cincinnati.

1978

I CAN'T BEAR TO LOOK!

Manager Don Zimmer's club, despite a 14½-game lead in August, loses Eastern Division title to New York in one-game playoff. Rice is AL's MVP with his league-leading 46 homers and 139 RBIs. Dennis Eckersley leads staff with 20 wins, while Mike Torrez goes 16–13.

1979

BEANTOWN BOMBERS!

Boston dips to third in AL East, despite Lynn's batting title with .333 average. He and Rice lead club with 39 homers, while Eckersley heads moundsmen with 17 wins. Torrez again goes 16–13 and Bob Stanley 16–12.

1981

THEY CALL ME "THE MAJOR"!

Ralph Houk is signed to manage Sox, and club finishes fifth in strike-interrupted season. Third baseman Carney Lansford leads AL with .336 average. Right fielder Dwight Evans shares AL homer title with 22. Torrez and Stanley each post 10 victories.

1982

I'M WADE-ING INTO A.L. PITCHING!

Houk brings Boston home third in East as rookie infielder Wade Boggs debuts with .349 average in 104 games. Evans paces club with 32 homers and 98 RBIs. Righty Mark Clear, with 14, is staff's top winner, while Eckersley and lefty John Tudor each win 13.

Despite Boggs's league-leading .361, Bosox sag to sixth in AL East. Rice leads league with 36 homers and 126 RBIs. Tudor,, 13–12, is their top winner, while Bruce Hurst and Bob Ojeda each win 12. Bob Stanley leads Sox with 33 saves.

Boston climbs to fourth, as outfielder Tony Armas leads AL with 43 homers and 123 RBIs. Pitching continues to be club problem, as Hurst, Ojeda, and Oil Can Boyd each go 12–12. Stanley paces club's relief corps with 22 saves. Rookie righty Roger Clemens goes 9–4.

Boggs's career-high .368 wins him his second AL batting title—the first of his four straight crowns. Evans leads club with 29 homers, and Rice is RBI leader with 103. Boyd goes 15–13, as Sox finish fifth under manager John McNamara.

Coach Joe Morgan replaces McNamara as manager in July, and Sox win AL East. Clemens and Bruce Hurst each win 18, while righty reliever Lee Smith chalks up 29 saves. Boggs's .366 wins batting crown. Boston, however, is eliminated in four straight by A's for AL flag.

Sox finish third in AL East despite 30 homers and 108 RBIs from first baseman Nick Esasky. Clemens wins 17 and righty Mike Boddicker 15. Smith again leads bullpen corps with 25 saves. Outfielder Mike Greenwell bats .308 with 14 homers and 95 RBIs.

Morgan wins another East title, but Sox are bounced in four straight by A's in flag showdown. Clemens goes 21–6 and leads AL with 1.93 ERA. Boggs's .302 leads Boston, while Ellis Burks paces club with 21 homers and 89 RBIs.

Sox take AL East with 95 wins, defeat Angels for AL flag, but lose seven-game World Series to New York Mets. Clemens is Cy Young and MVP winner on 24–4 season and league-leading 2.48 ERA. He strikes out record 20 batters in April game vs. Seattle. Boggs wins batting title with .357, while Boyd wins 16. Stanley saves 16 and lefty Joe Sambito saves 12.

California Angels

Gene Autry, famed Western film star and country-music singer, is granted expansion franchise, as American League invades West Coast. Bill Rigney, longtime skipper of Giants in New York and San Francisco, is named manager. Known as Los Angeles Angels, club finishes eighth in 10-club league, with best first-year showing of any expansion team (70–91, .435).

1961

I'M BACK IN THE SADDLE AGAIN...

Despite finishing third, 10 games behind Yankees, Angels challenge for pennant into September. Lefty Bo Belinsky no-hits Baltimore in May, and right-hander Dean Chance leads club with 14 wins, as club moves into brand-new Dodger Stadium as tenants of Dodgers.

1962 — *BO KNOWS NO-NOS!*

Chance wins 20 and Cy Young Award with his 1.65 ERA, the best in the American League. Chance and shortstop Jim Fregosi are club's All-Star Game starters at New York's Shea Stadium.

1964 — *THE CHANCE OF A LIFETIME!*

Fregosi, who leads Angels in batting (.277), hits (167), home runs (15), and RBIs (64), isn't reason why club sinks to seventh place. Pitching and defensive weaknesses help explain why Angels fail to contend in American League race.

1965 — *I EARNED MY HALO!*

Club shifts from Los Angeles to brand-new ballpark in Anaheim and is renamed California Angels. Joe Adcock leads Angels in homers (18), and lefty George Brunet and right-hander Jack Sanford each win 13 games.

1966 — *IT'S A HEAVENLY PLACE TO PLAY!* / *AMEN TO THAT!*

Lefty-swinging first baseman Don Mincher leads club in homers (25) and RBIs (76), as Angels finish fifth. Lack of plate punch by Mincher's teammates results in .238 club batting average, but the defense leads American League with .982 fielding percentage.

1967 — *YOU GUYS ARE WAY TOO ANGELIC TOWARDS THE OPPOSITION!*

Outfielder Rick Reichardt, whose $200,000 bonus was a record when he signed in 1964, leads club with .255 batting average and 21 homers. Continued failure of Angels to produce hits and runs help them sink to eighth place.

1968 — *OUR INVESTMENT IS PAYING DIVIDENDS!*

Baseball shifts to divisional play, and in late May, Harold (Lefty) Phillips replaces Rigney as manager with Angels in AL West basement. Club ends up in third but are 20 games below .500. Right-hander Andy Messersmith, with 16, is club's brightest mound prospect.

Another third-place windup, but this time Angels are 10 games above .500. Outfielder Alex Johnson wins the AL batting title with .329 average, the only Angel ever to claim that hitting prize. Clyde Wright contributes 22 victories, plus a no-hitter over Oakland on July 3.

Nolan Ryan joins Angels following deal with New York Mets, and he wins 19 and leads majors with 329 strikeouts.

Winkles is discharged in late June, and veteran skipper Dick Williams replaces him. Despite Ryan's 22 victories and 367 strikeouts, plus third career no-hitter, Angels plop into American League West basement.

Angels subscribe to running game and lead majors with 220 stolen bases, the most since 1916. Ryan, limited to 14 wins by elbow surgery, authors fourth no-hitter, and lefty Frank Tanana wins 16 and leads American League with 269 strikeouts.

Dick Williams is dismissed in late July, and coach Norm Sherry revives club sufficiently for them to finish tied for fourth with Texas. Ryan leads American League hurlers with 327 strikeouts.

Longtime Arizona State University baseball coach Bobby Winkles becomes manager. Ryan wins 21, pitches two no hitters, and sets major-league strikeout mark with 383, but Angels have to settle for fourth place. Right-hander Bill Singer, acquired from Dodgers, wins 20. Frank Robinson also comes from Los Angeles and hits 30 homers.

1979 — Fregosi guides Angels to American League West title, and designated hitter Don Baylor wins MVP as a result of his 36 homers and league-leading 139 RBIs. Free agent Rod Carew, seven-time American League batting champ with Twins, hits .318. Angels lose four-game American League Championship Series to Baltimore.

Autry's multimillion dollar investment in free agents Bobby Grich, Don Baylor, and Joe Rudi fail to pay early dividend when injuries doom Angels to fifth place. (Grich rebounds in subsequent years, and in February 1988 he is inducted into Angels' Hall of Fame.)

Autry favorite, Jim Fregosi, becomes manager, replacing Dave Garcia. The Angels win a club-record 87 games and finish tied for second with Texas.

Ryan goes to Houston via free agency. Angels sag to sixth when injuries sideline Baylor, Grich, Brian Downing, and Dan Ford, plus pitchers Bruce Kison and Dave Frost. Rod Carew hits .331.

Fregosi is canned in favor of Gene Mauch. Spending spree on free agents doesn't do it during strike-shortened season. Outfielder Fred Lynn, signed to four-year, $5.25 million contract responds with .219 batting average.

Reggie Jackson, signed as free agent, ties for American League homer lead with 39, and Angels zoom to top of American League West. Halos' pennant dream vanishes when they lose final three of best-of-five American League Championship Series playoff to Milwaukee.

Carew bats .339, and Lynn rebounds with 22 home runs, but uncertain pitching and injuries doom Cal to fifth-place tie in the American League West.

Angels tie Twins for second place. Jackson hits 25 homers, including 500th of his career, in September. Right-hander Mike Witt authors perfect game at Texas.

Mauch, who resigned in 1982, returns as manager to lead Angels to second, just one game behind Kansas City. Mike Witt leads moundsmen with 15 victories, and righty reliever Donnie Moore sets club mark with 31 saves.

Angels sink from top to bottom in American League West standings. Joyner hits 34 homers, but club loses 35 of final 54 games.

Mauch resigns during spring training, and Cookie Rojas is named skipper. Angels finish fourth, 12 games below .500. Pitching is again thin, and a season-ending, club-record 12-game losing streak punctuates the year.

Doug Rader is named manager, and club responds with third-place finish. Veteran right-hander Bert Blyleven wins 17 and pitches to 2.73 ERA while leading American League with five shutouts. Southpaw Jim Abbott, born without a right hand, wins 12, indicating his handicap is anything but.

Angels slide to fifth, with Finley the top winner at 18. Catcher Lance Parrish hits 24 homers, and Dave Winfield, acquired from Yankees, hits 21. Outfielder Luis Polonia, another ex-Yankee, hits .335.

Angels win West by five games and are one strike away from American League flag when disaster strikes. Boston rebounds to win final three of best-of-seven ALCS. Rookie first baseman Wally Joyner hits 22 homers, and veteran righty Don Sutton gets his 300th career win.

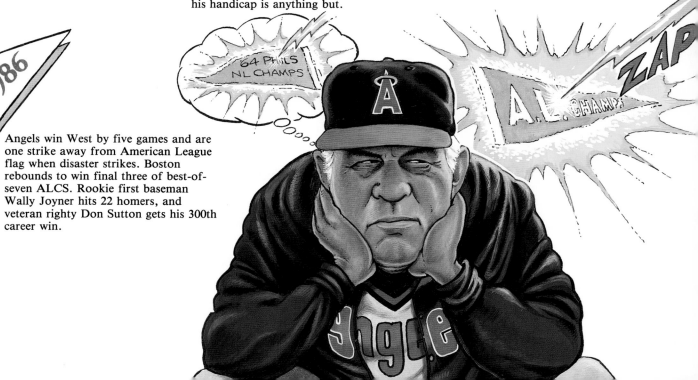

Chicago White Sox

The Year of the Black Sox stains Chisox's AL pennant, as eight members are later banned for "dumping" World Series against Cincinnati. Cicotte (29–7) and Lefty Williams (23–11) lead the staff. Jackson bats .351. The three are among the group banished by Commissioner Kenesaw Mountain Landis.

SAY IT AIN'T SO, JOE!

1919

1901

YES, THE WHITE STOCKINGS ARE NICE, BUT THEY DO GET QUITE DIRTY!

The White Stockings, as owner Charles A. Comiskey's club is called, wins AL's first pennant by four games over Boston. Right-hander Clark Griffith, serving as manager, wins 24 games and right-fielder Fielder Jones leads attack with .311 average.

1906

Sox bat a meager .230 and hit just seven home runs but win AL flag and defeat crosstown rival Cubs in World Series. Dubbed the "Hitless Wonders," Sox get superb pitching, with right-hander Frank Owen winning 22 and Nick Altrock 20.

1908

WALSH CANNOT LIVE BY PITCHING ALONE!!

Despite right-hander Ed Walsh's AL-leading 40-win season, Chisox finish third, 1½ games behind Detroit in tight three-team race. Club bats .224, and their three homers is AL mark for long-ball futility. Outfielder Patsy Dougherty, with .278, is club's leading hitter.

1910

OPEN FOR BUSINESS

COMISKEY PARK

White Sox finish sixth, but the big news is the brand-new ballpark they dedicate July 1. Known as Comiskey Park, it's baseball's finest arena and will house the club, in good times and bad, for the next 80 years.

1917

GIANT KILLERS!

Sox win AL flag by nine games, with a club-record 100 victories. They upend New York Giants in World Series. Right-hander Eddie Cicotte wins 28, while outfielder Happy Felsch bats .308 and outfielder Shoeless Joe Jackson hits .301.

1936

.388

After years of second-division finishes following the Black Sox scandal, Jimmy Dykes leads club to third place, its highest finish since 1920. Vern Kennedy wins 21 and future Hall of Famer Ted Lyons wins 10. Hall of Famer Luke Appling's .388 wins AL batting title.

Knuckleballer Eddie Fisher (15–7) and lefty Tommy John (14–7) are top winners for Lopez, always a master handler of pitchers. After third straight second-place windup, Lopez retires and the controversial Eddie Stanky becomes skipper.

Chuck Tanner leads Sox to second place in AL West, their best windup since 1965. Lefty knuckleballer Wilbur Wood's 24 wins tops AL. Stan Bahnsen goes 21–16, while first baseman Dick Allen is MVP with his 37 homers and 113 RBIs.

Wood again wins 24, but Sox staff and offense can't keep up, and club sags to fifth place. Third baseman Bill Melton and outfielder Carlos May each hit 20 homers, and Allen has .316 average and 16 homers.

White Sox finish fourth with 80–80 log, as lefty Jim Kaat wins 21 and Wood 20. Lefty Terry Forster chalks up 24 saves. Allen leads AL with 32 homers, and Melton hits 21. Second baseman Jorge Orta's .316 leads Sox at plate.

Tanner's managerial tenure ends with fifth place, and franchise is nearly moved to Seattle before being saved by Veeck's return and purchase in December. During season Kaat wins 20, and righty reliever Goose Gossage saves 26.

Paul Richards, a Veeck favorite, manages club to cellar windup. Lefty Ken Brett (10–12) is biggest winner, while first baseman Jim Spencer and Orta, now a right fielder, lead club with 14 homers. Lack of solid pitching doom Sox from outset.

Popular Bill Veeck purchases franchise, and Al Lopez skippers Sox to first flag since 1919. But Dodgers defeat Chi in six-game World Series. Righty Early Wynn (22–10) wins Cy Young Award. Veteran lefty Billy Pierce wins 14, and second baseman Nellie Fox is AL's MVP with .306 average.

1981

Club signs all-star catcher Carlton Fisk as free agent, and Sox advance to third. Designated hitter Greg Luzinski hits 21 homers and leads club with 62 RBIs. Pitching is club's strength, as Burns goes 10–6 while righty relievers LaMarr Hoyt and Farmer each save 10 games for manager Tony LaRussa.

1977

BOB'S OUR LEMON-AID

Bob Lemon becomes manager and hikes Chisox to third in AL West with 90 victories. Club hits 192 homers, as designated hitter Oscar Gamble slams 31, one more than left fielder Richie Zisk. Righty Steve Stone (15–12) heads mound corps.

1978

IT'S VEECK— HE SAYS ALL WE CAN AFFORD NOW ARE MIDGETS!

Free agency, plus Veeck's limited finances, cause Sox to tumble into fifth place in AL West. Third baseman Eric Soderholm's 20 homers leads club, while Stone wins 12 and reliever Lerrin La-Grow contributes 16 saves.

1979

COMISKEY PARK

DISCO INFERNO!

F.D.

A fifth-place finish results, as lefty Ken Kravec leads staff with 15 wins. Center fielder Chet Lemon's 17 homers tops offense. One of Sox's 87 defeats is July 12 forfeit to Detroit when Veeck's "Disco Demolition Night" promotion results in riot at Comiskey Park.

1980

THIS FARMER HARVESTED A BUMPER CROP OF SAVES!

Veeck's last year as owner passes with Sox landing in fifth, 20 games below .500. Lefty Britt Burns (15–13) leads moundsmen. Righty reliever Ed Farmer chalks up 30 saves. Infielder Jim Morrison and outfielder Wayne Nordhagen share homer lead with 15.

1982

HOYT'S HELPING US TO MAINTAIN OUR HEIGHT!

Another third-place windup is the result of Hoyt's 19–15 record as a starter, plus righty reliever Salome Barojas's 21 saves. Right fielder Harold Baines leads club with 25 homers and 105 RBIs. Luzinski socks 18 homers and knocks in 102.

1983

GIVING THE SOX A RON FOR THEIR MONEY!

KITTLE 42   35

Second-half spurt gives Sox AL West title by 20 games. Hoyt, Cy Young winner, goes 24–10, and right-hander Richard Dotson is 22–7. Righty reliever Dennis Lamp (15) and Barojas (12) produce the saves. Rookie of Year Ron Kittle hits 35 homers, but Sox lose pennant playoff to Baltimore.

Sox topple to fifth in AL West. Tom Seaver, drafted from Mets, goes 15–11 to top staff. Hoyt's 13–18 is sharp drop from previous year. Kittle leads club with 32 homers, and Baines (.304) hits 29, one of which wins AL record 25-inning marathon vs. Milwaukee in May.

Burns goes 18–11 and Seaver 16–11, including career win 300 on August 4 at Yankee Stadium. Despite .238 average, Fisk paces club with 37 homers. Baines bats .309 and has 113 RBIs. Shortstop Ozzie Guillen is AL Rookie of the Year.

LaRussa is axed in mid-June, as Sox stumble home fifth in AL West. Baines leads team with 21 homers, while DH Kittle hits 17. Pitching is the problem, as Joe Cowley posts 11–11, while Dotson and Floyd Bannister each win 10 while losing 17 and 14, respectively.

Jim Fregosi skippers Sox to another fifth-place windup, as Bannister's 16 victories heads staff. Righty reliever Bobby Thigpen produces 16 saves. Sox show some power as outfielder Ivan Calderon hits club-leading 28 homers, one more than first baseman Greg Walker.

Fregosi is dismissed following another fifth-place finish. Lefty Jerry Reuss (13–9) and righty Melido Perez (12–10) head starting staff. Thigpen saves 34. Outfielder Dan Pasqua heads Sox with 20 homers, one more than Fisk.

Jeff Torborg skippers Sox to last place in AL West, as the pitching is virtually nonexistent. Perez, 11–14, is biggest winner, but Thigpen continues to shine, saving 34. Calderon's 14 homers are the club high, while Fisk and Baines each hit 13.

Sox's final season at ancient Comiskey Park is huge success, as Torborg, AL Manager of the Year, brings them home second with 94 wins. Lefty Greg Hibbard and righty Jack McDowell each win 14, and Thigpen sets major-league record with 57 saves. Fisk leads club with 18 homers.

Cleveland Indians

1936 Right-hander Bob Feller, 17-year-old Iowa farmboy, debuts with fifth-place Tribe and launches Hall of Fame career. Lefty-hitting first baseman Hal Trosky enjoys career-high home runs (42) and batting average (.343) and leads American League with 162 RBIs.

1901 Cleveland, which hosted teams in the National League in the 1880s and 1890s, joins the newly minted American League. Nicknamed the Blues, they finish seventh. The following year they are joined by future Hall of Famer Napoleon (Nap) Lajoie.

1915 After employing a series of nicknames such as the Blues, Broncos, and Naps (for Lajoie), Cleveland formally adopts the name Indians. Despite Shoeless Joe Jackson's .331 average, in his final season in Cleveland, club finishes seventh.

1920 Following the promotion of Hall of Famer Tris Speaker to manager, the Tribe wins the AL flag and defeats Brooklyn in seven games in a best-of-nine World Series. Series features Elmer Smith's grand-slam homer and Bill Wambsganss's unassisted triple play.

1932 Indians play first game at brand-new 80,000-seat Municipal Stadium, July 31. Shift to Municipal isn't permanent until 1947 because club plays some games at 23,000-seat League Park. Right-hander Wes Ferrell wins more than 20 for fourth straight season.

1937 Right-hander Johnny Allen wins 15 straight but loses on final day to mar perfect record. Feller wins nine, as Tribe finishes fourth. Veteran right-hander Mel Harder, an Indian from 1928 to 1947, wins 15 en route to his lifetime total of 223 victories.

1940 Feller wins career-high 27, one being Opening Day no-hitter in Chicago. Indians finish one game behind Detroit for American League flag. Midseason player revolt against manager Oscar Vitt earns them label of "crybabies." Newspapers blast Indians for their attitude. Vitt isn't dismissed until season ends.

Indians, under Roger Peckinpaugh, finish fourth. Feller leads league with 25 wins, and pitchers Al Smith and Jim Bagby, Jr. combine to terminate Joe DiMaggio's 56-game hitting streak, July 17, in Cleveland. 24-year-old Lou Boudreau becomes "boy manager."

Gene Bearden and Bob Lemon each win 20, and Boudreau's team-leading .355 average earns him MVP. Indians take flag at Boston and then defeat Braves in World Series. Owner Bill Veeck brings Satchel Paige to Indians, and they draw all-time Cleveland high 2,620,000 fans.

An AL–record 111 victories give Indians the flag, but they lose World Series to New York Giants. Bobby Avila (.341) wins batting crown, while Lemon and Early Wynn each win 23. Outfielder Larry Doby paces American League with 32 homers and 126 RBIs.

Despite 16 wins and rookie-record 245 strikeouts from lefty Herb Score, Indians finish second to Yankees by three games. Lemon's 18 wins tie for American League lead. Outfielder Al Smith (.306) is Tribe's lone .300 hitter. Doby leads Indians with 26 homers, and Rosen's 81 RBIs top club.

Lopez's managerial career closes with another second-place windup despite Score's 20 wins and league-leading 263 strikeouts. Wynn and Lemon each win 20, and Feller ends 18-year career. Lefty-hitting first baseman Vic Wertz leads club with 32 homers and 106 RBIs.

Score's brilliant career is virtually ended in May when he is struck in right eye by line drive off bat of Yankees' Gil McDougald. Indians topple to sixth place. Wynn, going 14–17, is Cleveland's top winner.

Al Rosen hits an American League rookie-high 37 homers, as Indians finish fourth. Lemon leads league with 23 wins. Following the season, Boudreau is dismissed as skipper, and Al Lopez replaces him at the helm.

Birdie Tebbetts manages Tribe to fifth place, despite 17 wins from lefty Sam McDowell, whose 2.18 ERA leads league. The southpaw paces American League in strikeouts with 325 (his career high). It's the first of five strikeout titles he'll win in the next six seasons.

1965

IT'S THE "SUDDEN" SAM ERA!

1958

"ROCK" AND ROLL!

Bobby Bragan and Joe Gordon share managerial role, as Indians finish fourth. Right-hander Cal McLish (16) is staff's top winner, and outfielder Rocky Colavito's 41 homers are one behind Mickey Mantle's league-leading 42.

1960

THAT LANE IS CRAZY! I'M THE MANAGER, AND I JUST GOT TRADED!

Prior to Opening Day general manager "Frantic Frank" Lane swaps Colavito to Detroit for AL batting champion Harvey Kuenn. In August he ships manager Gordon to Detroit for Tigers' skipper Jimmy Dykes, the first time skippers have been "traded."

1968

IT'S THE BEGINNING OF THE DARK AGES!

Alvin Dark, in his first season as Cleveland skipper, leads Indians to third place. It is the highest the Tribe finishes in the 1960s. Right-hander Luis Tiant (21–9) leads American League with nine shutouts and 1.60 ERA. McDowell contributes 15 victories.

1970

FOSSE'S OUR ONLY RAY OF HOPE!

The decade of the 1970s, one in which Cleveland will see nothing but second-division finishes, opens with club fifth in six-team Eastern Division. McDowell (20–12) fans 304 in 305 innings. Sophomore catcher Ray Fosse leads club regulars with .307 average.

1975

POW!

Future Hall of Famer Frank Robinson becomes baseball's first black manager. Robinson, as designated hitter, homers in first at-bat on Opening Day. Club lands in fourth, and lefty Fritz Peterson (14) is top winning pitcher and Boog Powell is club home-run leader with 27.

1977

DANG!

Robinson is dismissed as manager in mid-June and replaced by coach Jeff Torborg. Tribe limps home in fifth place, as injuries to key personnel doom their season. Right-hander Wayne Garland, signed to a $2.3 million free-agent contract, injures shoulder and finishes 13–19.

For the sixth time in seven seasons, the Indians land in sixth place. A lack of pitching and defense mires club in second division. Right-hander Bert Blyleven is club's top winner with 19, while designated hitter Andre Thornton hits 33 homers and drives home 99.

The cellar-locked Tribe tie a club record with 102 losses, the most in majors. Lefty Neal Heaton (9–17) and Blyleven (9–11) pace staff in wins. Right-hander Tom Waddell, basically a reliever, wins eight and saves nine.

Cleveland wins 84 games, its highest total since 1968, while finishing in fifth place. Right fielder Joe Carter leads attack with .302 average, 29 homers, and league-leading 121 RBIs. Right-handed knuckleballer Tom Candiotti leads moundsmen with 16 victories.

Pitching, or lack of same, dooms Indians to 101 defeats and basement lease in American League East. Staff's 5.28 ERA is worst in majors. Right-handed reliever Doug Jones, 6–5 with eight saves, is the only hurler to win more than he loses.

Doc Edwards, in his first full season as manager, improves Tribe to sixth place in seven-club division with 78 wins. Lefty Greg Swindell (18–14) is staff leader, and Jones, with 37 saves, is ace of bullpen. Carter hits 27 homers, while Julio Franco bats .303.

When Indians slip to sixth, Edwards is dismissed as skipper, replaced by coach John Hart. Candiotti (13–10) and Swindell (13–6) are club's top winners, and Jones again stars out of bullpen with 32 saves. Carter, who is traded to San Diego in December, paces club with 35 homers and 105 RBIs.

Veteran manager John McNamara assumes Tribe's helm, and club responds with 77 victories and fourth place in the American League East. Candiotti (15–11) and Swindell (12–9) lead the club pitchers, and Jones produces 43 saves. Outfielder Candy Maldonado a free-agent pickup, hits career-high 22 homers, while catcher Sandy Alomar, Jr., wins American League Rookie of the Year Award.

Detroit Tigers

1905 Season's highlight was September arrival of 18-year-old rookie Ty Cobb. The Georgia Peach will star with Tigers through 1926, and many still deem him to be the greatest player of all time. Right-hander Ed Killian is club's top winner with 23 victories.

WE'LL CLAW OUR WAY TO THE TOP!

1901 Detroit, which fielded a club in the National League in the 1880s, becomes a charter member of the American League. With George Stallings, whose 1890s' team were nicknamed the Tigers, as manager, Detroit finishes third in the eight-club circuit.

WE'RE GONNA REPEAT—THEN, THREE-PEAT!

1907 Cobb bats .350 and wins the first of his 12 American League batting titles (nine in a row), as manager Hughie Jennings wins first of three straight American League flags. In World Series, Tigers lose four straight to Chicago Cubs after 3–3 tie in opener halted by darkness.

WAHOO! SEVEN HOMERS! THAT'LL SCARE THEM CUBS!

1908 Cobb takes batting title with .324, and future Hall of Famer Sam Crawford leads league with seven homers. Rookie Ed (Kickapoo Chief) Summers leads staff with 24 victories. Tigers win flag by half a game over Cleveland but again bow to Cubs in World Series.

THIS IS NOT THE SORT OF "THREE-PEAT" THAT A MANAGER DREAMS OF!

1909 Right-hander George Mullin leads American League with 29 victories, and Cobb wins Triple Crown (.377 batting average, nine homers, and 107 RBIs). Detroit wins flag by 3½ over Philadelphia but for third straight year loses World Series, this one in seven games to Pirates.

HEY! HE STOLE MY BASE — AGAIN!

1915 Tigers, despite winning 100 games, finish 2½ games behind Red Sox in American League race. Cobb hits .369 and steals 96 bases, a one-season record that will stand for 47 years. Right-hander George Dauss and left-hander Harry Coveleski win 24 and 22 games, respectively.

.394 — ALL HAIL HEILMANN!

1921 Cobb becomes manager, and Tigers end up in sixth place. Outfielder Harry Heilmann bats .394 and leads league. It's first of four batting crowns he'll win through 1927, taking title in odd-number years.

24

Mickey Cochrane, A's star catcher, becomes manager and leads club to first flag since 1909. Schoolboy Rowe wins 24 and Tommy Bridges 22. Greenberg, Goslin, and Gehringer—contribute mightily at the plate. Detroit loses World Series to St. Louis Cardinals.

Tigers win first world championship in club's history, defeating Chicago Cubs in six-game World Series. Greenberg leads American League with 170 RBIs, and his 36 homers tie for title. Bridges wins 21 games, plus two more in World Series.

Cochrane, whose playing career ended as result of serious beaning in May 1937, is replaced as skipper in August. Tigers finish fourth, but Greenberg captures headlines with 58-homer season in which he challenges Babe Ruth's record of 60.

Bobo Newsom wins 21, and Greenberg leads AL with 41 homers and 150 RBIs, as Tigers win flag by game over Cleveland when right-hander Floyd Giebell defeats Indians' ace Bob Feller in one of only three major-league games he ever won. Season is marred by Tigers' seven-game World Series loss to Cincinnati.

Lefty Hal Newhouser wins MVP for second straight year, as he posts 25 wins (54 in two seasons). Greenberg returns from army and helps win flag with grand-slam homer in September. Newhouser wins two games in Tigers' seven-game World Series triumph over Cubs.

Bob Scheffing's club wins 101 games but finishes second to New York Yankees, winners of 109. Lefty-hitting Norm Cash leads American League with .361 average. Outfielder Rocky Colavito hits 45 homers, and right-hander Frank Lary wins 23 to pace Detroit's moundsmen.

After missing pennant by one game in 1967, manager Mayo Smith guides Tigers to 12-length romp in American League flag race. Willie Horton leads club with 36 homers, and right-hander Denny McLain wins 31, the first American League pitcher to do so in 37 years. Tigers, with lefty Mickey Lolich winning three games, upset Cardinals in seven-game World Series.

1974 Ralph Houk launches his five-year tenure as Tigers' manager, but club sags to Eastern Division cellar. Season is farewell for future Hall of Famer Al Kaline. The veteran outfielder, who never played in minors, finishes 22-season career in Detroit with 3,007 base hits.

1972 HEY, LIGHTEN UP, YOU'RE WINNING!

Cash hits 22 homers, and Lolich wins 22, as Billy Martin skippers Tigers to Eastern Division title. They lose playoff in five to A's in which Oakland's Bert Campaneris draws suspension when he throws bat at Lerrin Lagrow after being hit by a pitch in Game 2.

1976 YOU'RE A STRIKE... REMEMBER?

Mark (The Bird) Fidrych wins 19 for fifth-place Bengals. His colorful antics—and ability to retire opposing hitters—earn him Rookie of the Year Award. Outfielder Ron LeFlore leads club with .316 average, and designated hitter Rusty Staub leads team in RBIs (96).

1977

Tigers achieve fourth place, but season is ill-fated when Fidrych tears knee cartilage in spring training. Arm problems soon force him out of baseball. LeFlore leads team with .325, and first baseman Jason Thompson paces it in homers (31).

1978 ♫ SIDE-BY-SIDE! ♫

Houk concludes with fifth-place finish. Shortstop Alan Trammell and second baseman Lou Whitaker, Rookie of the Year, begin a double-play combination that is to exist into the 1990s. Staub, the DH, hits two dozen homers, and his 121 RBIs are the most by a Tiger player since 1961.

1979 THIS TEAM JUST NEEDS THE RIGHT KIND OF SPARKY!

Sparky Anderson becomes manager in mid-June. The arrival of Anderson, who enjoyed longtime success as Cincinnati pilot, buoys Tiger fans. Sophomore righty Jack Morris wins 17.

1983 AHH... SWEET MUSIC!

Anderson and the Tigers start putting it together and finish second behind Baltimore. Morris wins 20 and right-hander Dan Petry 19. Aurelio Lopez, known as Señor Smoke, has 18 saves. Whitaker, Trammell, first baseman Enos Cabell, and outfielder Larry Herndon are the .300 hitters.

When Tigers win nine straight one of them a no-hitter by Morris, they are off to club-record 104 wins and the AL flag. Reliever Willie Hernandez saves 32 and wins the AL's MVP and Cy Young awards. Bengals win it all with triumph over San Diego in World Series.

The Tigers dip to third, but Evans and Hernandez aren't the reasons why. Evans, at 38, becomes the oldest ever to lead the AL in homers when he hits 40, and Hernandez has 31 saves. Kirk Gibson chips in with 29 homers and 97 RBIs, while Morris wins 16.

Morris wins 21 and Hernandez saves two dozen, but the Tigers again land in third place. Six Tigers hit 20 or more homers, with Evans's 29 heading the club's four-base list.

Detroit wins AL East by two games over Toronto, and Anderson gains Manager of the Year honors. Trammell, with .343 batting mark, paces Tigers' regulars, and his 105 RBIs lead the team. Evans's 34 homers are the club high. The Tigers lose to Minnesota in AL playoff.

Tigers lose the Eastern Division title to Boston by one game. Trammell (.311) is Detroit's lone .300 batter. Right-hander Mike Henneman leads the staff with 22 saves. Morris (15) wins the most games, and Evans, with 22, leads in home runs.

The bottom falls out, and the Tigers crash into the American League East basement, losing 103 games in the process. Detroit doesn't have a starter with a winning record. Whitaker, with 28 homers, has the biggest bat in the Tigers' impotent attack.

Outfielder Cecil Fielder, a former Toronto player whom Detroit signs as a free agent from Japanese baseball, hits 51 homers and has 132 RBIs, as Tigers rebound to third place. Fielder's league-leading homer total is most by a Tiger player since Greenberg's 58 in 1938.

Kansas City Royals

Royals win first of three straight AL West titles, but pennant vanishes when Yankees win best-of-five playoff. Brett's .333 gives him his first AL batting title, and designated hitter Hal McRae hits .332. Righty Dennis Leonard (17–10) is top winner, and reliever Mark Littell saves 16.

Kansas City is readmitted to the American League via an expansion franchise. Majors go to divisional play, and Royals finish fourth in six-club Western Division. Righty Wally Bunker wins 12, while Dick Drago and Moe Drabowsky each win 11.

Club moves into brand-new Royals Stadium, a 40,000-seat, artificial-turf arena, and win 88 games to land in second in AL West. Fans get 13-game look at George Brett. John Mayberry and Amos Otis lead club with 26 homers, while Paul Splittorff goes 20–11.

Whitey Herzog becomes manager in late July and leads Royals to second place with 91 victories. Brett's .308 average tops club, while Mayberry sets pace with 34 homers and 106 RBIs. Steve Busby, who pitched no-hitters in 1973 and 1974, tops staff with 18 wins.

A club-high 102 victories win division, but again Yankees take the pennant. Leonard wins 20 and Splittorff 16. Right-hander Doug Bird wins 11 and saves 14. Brett and outfielder Al Cowens each hit .312, but latter outhomers Brett, 23–22.

Yet another division, but also another playoff setback by the Yankees. Leonard posts 21 victories, Splittorff 19. Lefty Larry Gura contributes 16, and lefty reliever Al Hrabosky saves 20. Otis leads regulars with .298 average, 22 homers, and 96 RBIs.

Freshman skipper Jim Frey leads Royals to AL flag, but they bow to Philadelphia in six-game World Series. Brett's .390 wins him batting crown, plus MVP honors. Leonard goes 20–11, Gura 18–10, and Dan Quisenberry posts 33 saves.

Despite winning Western Division in strike-interrupted season, under manager Dick Howser, Royals lose three straight to Oakland in divisional playoff. Brett, following dismal start, bats .314, while Leonard wins 13 and Gura 11. Quisenberry, the relief ace, saves 18.

The famed "pine tar" game, July 24 at Yankee Stadium. Brett hits ninth-inning homer to give Kansas City 5–4 lead, but Yankees' protest—that his bat contains "pine tar" higher than the 18 inches allowed—is upheld by umpires. AL president Lee MacPhail subsequently reverses umpires' decision.

Dick Howser skippers Royals to Western Division title, but Detroit beats them for AL pennant. Switch-hitting center fielder Willie Wilson's .301 leads regulars, and righty-hitting first baseman Steve Balboni clouts 28 homers. Lefty Bud Black tops staff with 17 wins, and Quisenberry registers 44 saves.

Royals, under Howser, win it all, including seven-game upset of Cardinals in World Series. Cy Young Award winner Bret Saberhagen goes 20–6, while Charlie Leibrandt wins 17 and Quisenberry has 37 saves. Balboni leads team with 36 homers, while Brett hits 30 and bats .335.

1989 Saberhagen is AL ERA leader at 2.16, goes 23–6, and wins Cy Young prize, as Royals finish second. Jackson paces lineup with 32 homers and 105 RBIs and gains national recognition in All-Star Game at Anaheim. Royals do all this without a .300 hitter in their lineup.

A STAR IS BORN!

ALL-STAR MVP

1986 Royals sinks to third, as Howser is fatally striken by brain tumor. Club doesn't have a .300 batter in lineup, but Balboni leads them with 29 homers. Pitching comes up short, as Leibrandt tops staff with 14 wins, and Quisenberry's saves slip to mere 12.

WELL, AT LEAST WE GOT OUR SEITZER ON THIRD!

...AND WE'VE GOT OUR SIGHTS ON FIRST!

1987 KC settles for second in AL West. Right-hand-hitting third baseman Kevin Seitzer leads club with .323 average and league-high 207 hits. Outfielder Danny Tartabull slams club-leading 34 homers and 101 RBIs. Saberhagen tops staff with 18 wins, two more than Leibrandt.

MARK MY WORDS, THE ROYALS WILL REIGN AGAIN!

1988 Royals slide to third, as right-hander Mark Gubicza goes 20–8, and righty reliever Steve Farr chalks up 20 saves. Brett, now a first baseman, leads regulars with .306 average, and Tartabull's 26 homers are one more than football star Bo Jackson delivers.

I LIKE TO WIN A BATTING CROWN EVERY DECADE OR SO!

.329

1990 Royals drop all the way to sixth despite Brett's league-leading .329 average. Jackson, limited to 111 games, leads club with 28 homers. Farr's 13 wins is best on staff, but rookie righty Kevin Appier and fellow righty Tom Gordon each win 12 games.

Milwaukee Brewers

1978 Manager George Bamberger hikes Brewers to third place in AL East, as Mike Caldwell goes 22–9 and Lary Sorensen wins 18. Left fielder Larry Hisle leads club with 34 homers and 115 RBIs, while outfielder Gorman Thomas socks 32 homers and drives in 86 runs.

WE'VE GOT SOMETHING BREWING!

1970 WE'LL TRY TO MAKE OL' MILWAUKEE FAMOUS ONCE AGAIN!

AL transfers Seattle franchise to Milwaukee, which lost the NL Braves after 1965. Named the Brewers, the team ties for fourth with Kansas City in AL West. Tommy Harper leads team with .296 average and 31 homers. Marty Pattin leads staff with 14 victories.

1972 GEE, I DON'T THINK WE'RE IN KANSAS ANYMORE! NO, IT'S THE A.L. EAST!

The AL's realignment transfers Milwaukee to the Eastern Division, but the change is also a second straight basement windup for the Brewers. Jim Lonborg's 14 wins tops staff which gets little help from an offense that fails to produce even a .300 hitter.

1974 HE'S JUST A KID! HOW LONG DO YOU FIGURE HE'LL LAST?

Brewers again land in fifth, as 18-year-old shortstop Robin Yount launches career. Veteran third baseman Don Money leads lineup with .283 average, while Scott and outfielder John Briggs lead club with 17 homers apiece. Right-hander Jim Slaton (13–16) is staff leader.

1975 GREAT SCOTT!

Righty first baseman George Scott leads AL with 36 homers and 109 RBIs, as Brewers land fifth. Pitching is problem, however, and staff's 4.34 ERA is highest in AL. Pete Brober (14–16) is biggest winner. Reliever Tom Murphy, despite 1–9 record, saves 20 games.

Brewers win AL East and AL flag in playoff with Angels but drop World Series to Cardinals. Harvey Kuenn is named manager in June, Brewers' Thomas ties for AL homer lead with 39. Yount (.331) wins MVP, and Vuckovich (18–6) gets Cy Young.

Milwaukee topples to fifth despite Cecil Cooper's league-leading 126 RBIs. He also bats .307 and hits 30 homers. Yount and catcher Ted Simmons co-lead club with .308 averages. Righty Moose Haas goes 13–3, though Slaton's 14 wins pace staff.

Brewers land in AL East cellar, and 39-year-old right-hander Don Sutton (14–12) is only starter with winning record. Fingers, however, does save 23. Club doesn't own a .300 hitter, though Yount leads team with .298, 16 homers, and 80 RBIs.

Milwaukee reaches sixth place. Rookie lefty Ted Higuera goes 15–8, and he's only hurler to win more than he loses. Future Hall of Famer Fingers, in his final season, saves 17 and is No. 1 save artist, with 341 lifetime. Cooper leads team with 16 homers, while Yount, an outfielder now, hits 15.

Strike-shortened season. Milwaukee wins second half of East race but drops best-of-five divisional playoff to Yankees. Righty Pete Vuckovich paces staff with 14 wins, and righty reliever Rollie Fingers saves 28 and gets Cy Young Award. Outfielder Gorman Thomas hits 21 homers, tops on squad.

YOUNT ON THE MOUNT!

1989

Milwaukee plays .500 ball but slips to fourth in AL East. Righty Chris Bosio (15–10) is staff's best. A back problem limits Higuera to 22 starts and 9–6 record. Plesac has 33 saves. Yount's .318 and 103 RBIs earns him American League MVP.

MVP

1986

HAVE WE GOT A UNIFORM THAT'LL FIT A GIANT DEER ?!?

Brewers retain sixth place, as Higuera goes 20–11. Outfielder Rob Deer, acquired from Giants, leads Brewers with 33 homers and 86 RBIs. Yount's .312 average is team's best, and he's Brewer's lone .300 batsman.

1987

WE'RE HAPPY WITH HIGUERA, NUTS ABOUT NIEVES, WILD OVER WEGMAN AND PLEASED WITH PLESAC!

ROSTER

Milwaukee's revised roster responds with third-place finish, as Higuera wins 18, righty Juan Nieves 14, and Bill Wegman a dozen. Reliever Dan Plesac saves 23. Yount's .312 leads club, and Deer's 28 homers are team tops. Dale Sveum, in first full season, hits 25 home runs.

1988

MOLITOR .312

Brewers again finish third, tied with Toronto. Deer leads squad with 23 homers. Paul Molitor leads lineup with .312 average. Yount hits .306 and leads squad with 91 RBIs. Higuera (16–9) is staff leader, while rookie righty Dan August wins 13, as does Wegman. Plesac contributes 30 saves.

1990

THIS BREW HAS GONE FLAT!

WHIFF!

Brewers sag to sixth and fail to field a .300 hitter. Deer, with 27, again leads club in homers, and 38-year-old DH Dave Parker, a free-agent signee, heads club's RBI list with 92. Pitching is the problem. Righty Ron Robinson's 12–5 is staff high. Higuera goes 11–10, and Plesac has 24 saves.

Minnesota Twins

1912 Clark Griffith begins 43-year association with Washington when he becomes 10% owner and Senators' manager. He guides club to second place, as Johnson wins 32. Griffith institutes policy of President throwing out ball on Opening Day.

THANK YOU, MR. PRESIDENT!

1901 *DOORMATS NO MORE!*

Washington, whose clubs were National League also-rans in the 1890s, is granted a franchise in fledgling American League and finishes sixth in the eight-club circuit. Lefty Casey Patten, with 18 wins, is team's best hurler.

1907 *WASHINGTON... FIRST IN THE HEARTS OF AMERICANS AND LAST IN THE AMERICAN LEAGUE!*

Senators finish last, but high spot is deebut of 19-year-old Walter Johnson. Future Hall of Fame right-hander launches 21-season career-winning five games. Club loses 102, and no pitcher posts a winning record.

1924 *BUCKY HARRIS, BOY MANAGER!*

Manager Bucky Harris, at 27, leads Senators to first flag and a World Series win over New York Giants. Harris, in 29 seasons as a skipper, will guide Senators on three occasions. Johnson wins 23, and Goose Goslin leads AL with 129 RBIs.

1925 *GOOSE ON THE LOOSE!*

Senators repeat as flag winners but lose seven-game World Series to Pittsburgh after leading three games to one. Righty Stan Coveleski and Johnson each win 20 games, and future Hall of Famer Goslin paces club with 18 homers and 113 RBIs.

1933 *I'M ONLY JOE! —NOT DAVID!*

Shortstop Joe Cronin, at 26, is another of Griffith's "boy" managers, and he wins AL flag in first term at helm. Club, however, loses World Series to Giants in five. Right-hander Alvin Crowder paces AL with 24 victories, and lefty Earl Whitehill wins 22. Four of Cronin's regulars bat .300 or better.

1961

When AL expands to 10 clubs, Senators, now operated by Calvin Griffith, Clark's adopted son, transfer franchise to Minneapolis–St. Paul and are renamed Minnesota Twins. After last flag in 1933, they had only four first-division finishes in final 27 years at Griffith Stadium.

Twins vault from sixth place in 1964 to AL pennant under Sam Mele, winning 102 games. But they lose Series in seven games to Los Angeles Dodgers. Righty Mudcat Grant leads AL with 21 wins, and lefty Jim Kaat wins 18. Tony Oliva wins AL batting title with .321 average.

Twins, under Bill Rigney, repeat in AL West but again are wiped out by Orioles in flag playoff. Perry leads AL with 24 wins and lefty reliever Ron Perranoski saves 34. Killebrew leads Twins with 41 homers and 113 RBIs.

Despite Oliva's league-leading .337 average, Twins sink to fifth in AL West. Perry goes 17-17 and Bert Blyleven 16-15 as sophomore. Twins' bullpen springs a leak, and lefty Tom Hall is top save artist with nine.

Carew's .318 leads AL, the first of four straight hit titles for the Panamanian native. Twins, however, finish third. Blyleven wins 17, and righty reliever Wayne Granger saves 19. Killebrew, as usual, leads club with 26 homers.

Blyleven wins 20, and Carew's .350 is AL tops, as Minny plays .500 and again lands third. Right-handed hitting outfielder Bobby Darwin leads them with 18 homers. Righty bullpenner Ray Corbin is top reliever with 14 saves.

Third place is again Twins' home, as Killebrew hits 13 homers in his Minnesota farewell. Blyleven (17-17) is top winner and righty Joe Decker goes 16-14. Carew leads majors with .364 average, but he's only Twin regular to hit .300.

Baseball expands to 12-team leagues and adopts divisional play. Billy Martin leads Twins to AL West but loses playoff to Baltimore for AL flag. Righties Dave Boswell and Jim Perry each win 20. Harmon Killebrew leads AL in homers (49) and RBIs (140). Rod Carew hits .332 to win first of seven AL batting titles.

A TWIN'S PEAKS!

.388 MVP

1977

Despite Carew's league-leading .388, his career high, plus 28 homers and league-leading 119 RBIs from outfielder Larry Hisle, Twins land fourth. Right-hander Dave Goltz wins 20, and righty reliever Tom Johnson goes 16–7, with 15 saves.

1976

CAMPBELL IS HMM..HMM.. ...GREAT!

WINS SAVES

Twins enjoy best season in six years, as they win 85 games and finish third in AL West. Carew (.331) and outfielder Lyman Bostock (.323) pace club at plate, and Dan Ford hits 20 homers. Righty reliever Bill Campbell wins 17 and saves 20 others.

1978

HOME OF 4TH PLACE

METROPOLITAN STAD

Another fourth-place windup, this one 16 games below .500. Carew leads AL with .333 before taking free-agent deal from California Angels. Goltz leads Twins' staff with 15 wins, while righty Roger Erickson and lefty Geoff Zahn each win 14.

1979

THIS LEFTY STILL HAS SOME PITCHING LEFT!

20

Twins again finish fourth, and veteran lefty Jerry Koosman, a free-agent signee from Mets, goes 20–13. Goltz wins 14 and Zahn 13, while righty reliever Mike Marshall chalks up 32 saves. Shortstop Roy Smalley leads club with 24 homers and 95 RBIs.

1980

WELL, I'VE JUST HAD TOO MAUCH OF THIS FOURTH-PLACE STUFF!

MANAGER

Gene Mauch, Twins' skipper since 1976, resigns in August, and club ends up in third, 19½ behind Kansas City. Koosman (16–13) is top winner and only starter above .500. Right-hander Doug Corbett heads bullpen with 23 saves.

1981

THERE WAS A PLAYER'S STRIKE? I DIDN'T NOTICE!!

Twins' pitching and power disappear, and club settles into AL West cellar in strike-shortened season. Right-hander Pete Redfern (9–8) is top winner, but Corbett manages 17 saves. Smalley's seven homers is team high.

1982

OOPS! SORRY!

RIPP!

Twins move into domed stadium in downtown Minneapolis, but 102 losses keep them in basement. Lefty-hitting first baseman Kent Hrbek hits 23 homers and has 92 RBIs as rookie. Righty Bobby Castillo's 13 wins tops staff, while righty Ron Davis saves 22.

Griffith family ends 72-year connection with club when club is sold to local group headed by Carl Pohlad. Twins play .500 and reach third place. Tom Brunansky hits 32 homers. Frank Viola wins 18 and Mike Smithson 15. Davis contributes 29 saves.

Minny dips to fourth place despite 18 victories from Viola and 15 from Smithson. Blyleven returns after nine seasons in both leagues and wins eight. Davis saves 25. Brunansky paces attack with 27 HRs, while Hrbek's 93 RBIs lead club.

Tom Kelly manages club to World Series upset win over St. Louis. Club wins AL West by two over Kansas City, then defeats Detroit in flag playoff. Viola wins 17 and Blyleven 15, while bullpen star Jeff Reardon saves 31. Puckett hits .332; Hrbek 34 HRs.

Viola leads AL with 24 victories, and Puckett hits .356, but Twins finish second, 13 behind Oakland. Gaetti leads club with 28 homers, three more than Hrbek, who bats .312. Reardon dominates pen with 42 saves.

Twins finish fifth, two games below .500, despite Puckett's league-leading .339 average. Viola goes 8–12 before being dealt to Mets. Lefty Allan Anderson leads staff with 17 wins, and Reardon saves 31.

Club slides into AL West basement, as pitching falters. Righty Kevin Tapani is tops with 12 wins, but Anderson slumps to 7–18. Righty Rick Aguilera, who replaces Reardon in pen, saves 32. Puckett's average is .298, while Hrbek hits 22 homers.

Twins land in sixth, but rotund outfielder Kirby Puckett achieves stardom with .328 average, plus 31 homers and 96 RBIs. Third baseman Gary Gaetti leads club with 34 homers and 108 RBIs. Blyleven wins 17. Viola (16–13) is other Minny hurler to win more than he loses.

New York Yankees

1927 Ruth sets one-season home-run record of 60. Yankees win 110 games to take American League flag by 19 games over Philadelphia A's. Bombers upend Pittsburgh in four straight Series sweep to earn "greatest team ever" accolade.

1904 The Yankees, despite a record 41 victories by Jack Chesbro, lose flag to Boston on season's final day when the right-hander uncorks a tie-breaking wild pitch in ninth inning against the Red Sox. Their 92 victories are the most a Yankees' club will achieve until 1920.

1920 Yankees purchase Babe Ruth from Boston in a quarter million dollar deal. Playing his home games at New York's Polo Grounds, Ruth hammers a record 54 home runs. Yankees finish third in tight race behind Cleveland and Chicago.

1921 Ruth hits 59 home runs and drives in 171 as Yankees win first of their record 33 AL pennants. Miller Huggins directs club to the first of his six flags, and right-hander Carl Mays chalks up 27 victories. Season is spoiled when rival Giants down Yankees in World Series.

1923 Yankees move into brand-new Yankee Stadium, known as "House That Ruth Built," and the Babe christens arena by hitting Opening Day homer vs. Boston. Yankees win third straight pennant and capture first of record 22 World Championships when they defeat Giants in World Series.

1925 Babe Ruth's famed "stomache ache" and late-season suspension help doom Yankees to seventh-place finish. Lou Gehrig launches his iron-man streak of playing in 2,130 consecutive games.

1931 Joe McCarthy, who never played in majors, is named Yankees' manager. The club, despite Gehrig's American League record of 184 RBIs, finishes second, 13½ behind Philadelphia. Ruth and Gehrig tie for American League homer title with 46, and Lefty Gomez, in his first full season, wins 21 games.

McCarthy guides Yankees to first of eight pennants and seven World Series he'll win as manager. With five regulars hitting .300 or better, Bombers outdistance A's by 13 games. Ruth hits famous "called shot" homer vs. Charlie Root in four-game Series sweep of Cubs.

The aging Ruth plays his final season in New York. Yankees, despite Gomez's career-high 26 wins and Gehrig's Triple Crown performance of leading the American League in batting (.363), home runs (49), and RBIs (165), finish second, seven games behind Detroit.

Gehrig's career ends when he retires after 2,130 straight appearances. Iron Horse has an illness which takes his life two years later. On July 4, Gehrig makes "luckiest man on face of the earth" speech. Yankees win flag by 17 and obliterate Cincinnati in World Series.

McCarthy, without an American League pennant since 1943, resigns in May. In September, with club en route to third-place windup, future Hall of Famer Yogi Berra joins club.

Casey Stengel is named skipper and wins the first of his record five straight World Series. Yankees win pennant, defeating Boston twice in season's final weekend, then defeat Brooklyn in five-game Series.

Allie Reynolds, a 17-game winner, pitches two no-hitters, over Cleveland and Boston. Rookie Mickey Mantle arrives in April, and veteran Joe DiMaggio retires after six-game Series win over Giants in October.

1941

Joe DiMaggio hits in record 56 straight games from May 15 to July 16. Yankees cop American League pennant by 17 games. They frost the cake in World Series, downing Brooklyn Dodgers in five games.

56

ROGER —AND OUT!

STOTTLEMYRE IS DOIN' A MEL OF A JOB!

Mantle's .353 batting average, 52 homers, and 130 RBIs win Triple Crown and American League's MVP prize. Lefty Whitey Ford's 2.47 earns him ERA title. In seven-game Series win over Dodgers, right-hander Don Larsen pitches perfect game in Game 5 at Yankee Stadium.

Stengel, who won 10 pennants and seven World Series, retires. Roger Maris sets one-season home-run record with 61, eclipsing Ruth's 34-year-old mark. Whitey Ford wins career-high 25 games. Yankees top season with five-game World Series win over Cincinnati.

Houk, after three straight World Series titles, becomes general manager, and Yogi Berra is named manager. Mel Stottlemyre joins in August and wins nine games to help win flag over Chicago. Berra is dismissed following Series loss to Cardinals.

Yankees finish second to Baltimore, their best season since 1964. Catcher Thurman Munson's .302 batting average earns him Rookie of the Year honors. Outfielder Bobby Murcer, unfairly billed as the "new Mantle," contributes 23 home runs.

Cleveland shipbuilder George M. Steinbrenner III heads group that purchases Yankees from CBS in January. Houk, who resumed managing team in 1966, resigns amid rumors that differences with Steinbrenner prompted decision.

I'M HIRED! I'M FIRED! I'M HIRED! I'M FIRED? I'M HIRED!...

Yankee Stadium undergoes two-year renovation, and club moves into Shea Stadium as tenants of the Mets. Steinbrenner, though under a two-year suspension by Commissioner Bowie Kuhn, steals headlines when he signs free agent Jim "Catfish" Hunter on New Year's Eve.

Billy Martin becomes Yankees' manager in August. It's the first of five different times he'll skipper the ballclub. Hunter wins 23, Bobby Bonds bops 32 homers, Munson hits .318 and drives in 102 runs.

1977

Free agent Reggie Jackson signs rich five-year contract and begins starry and stormy career with Yankees. He hits 32 homers and drives in 110 runs despite dugout fistfight with manager Martin at Boston in June. Yankees win Series against Dodgers, and Jackson dominates with record-tying three home runs in Game 6.

1976

Yankees return to refurbished Stadium and win pennant on Chris Chambliss's ninth-inning homer in final game of Championship vs. KC. Munson is AL's MVP, and Nettles leads league with 32 homers. Cincinnati defeats Yankees in four straight in World Series.

1978

Yankees, 13½ games behind Boston in August, rebound to win Division title on Bucky Dent's three-run homer in one-game playoff at Boston. Guidry goes 25-3 and wins Cy Young. Club defeats Dodgers in six games for Series title.

1981

Dave Winfield signs multimillion dollar contract. Club honors the late Elston Howard, the Yankees first black and league MVP. Yankees win first half of AL East in split season and defeat Milwaukee and Oakland to gain World Series. They lose to Dodgers.

1984

First baseman Don Mattingly, playing his first full season, wins American League batting title with a .323 average, besting teammate Winfield by three points on season's final day.

1986

FROM RAGS... TO RICHES!

Manager Lou Piniella guides club to second place behind Boston. Pitching star is lefty Dave Righetti, who authored 1983 no-hitter as starter. Coming out of bullpen, he wins eight and sets relief record with 46 saves. Mattingly, the American League's MVP in 1985, bats .352 with 31 homers and 113 RBIs.

1990

HOW IN THE WORLD DID I LOSE A NO-NO?!?

Andy Hawkins pitches no-hitter at Chicago on July 1—but is second man in 20th century to lose hitless effort, as White Sox win, 4-0. George Steinbrenner, principal owner, is ordered by Baseball Commissioner Fay Vincent to step down as Yankees' boss. Yankees, never in the race, sink into American League East cellar.

Oakland A's

1931

A's win third straight AL flag but lose World Series to St. Louis in seven games. Simmons's .390 leads AL batsmen. Grove (31–4) wins ERA title (2.06) and is AL's MVP. Mack, a victim of the Depression, begins selling off his best players.

A REAL TROPHY OF A SEASON!

1901

Philadelphia becomes a charter member of the AL when Connie Mack and sporting-goods manufacturer Ben Shibe are granted a franchise. The A's, with Hall of Famer Nap Lajoie in his lone Philly season, finish fourth. Lajoie leads AL with .422 average.

1905

LEFTY POWER!

Mack's club wins flag, their second in four years, but lose five-game World Series to New York Giants. Lefty Eddie Plank (25–12) and fellow southpaw Rube Waddell (26–11) lead staff. First baseman Harry Davis leads AL with, believe it or not, eight homers.

1911

$100,000! FOR ALL THAT MONEY, DO WE HAVE TO TAKE CARE OF THE LAWN, TOO?

A's win second straight flag and World Series, as Mack's $100,000 infield of McInnis, Collins, Barry, and Baker combine for .323 batting average. Righties Jack Coombs (28–12) and Albert (Chief) Bender (17–5), plus Plank's 23 wins, give A's superior pitching.

1914

A's win third flag in four years but are upset in four by Boston Braves in World Series. Baker's nine homers leads league, while Bob Shawkey and Bullet Joe Bush each win 16 games. Management begins dismantling club, and moves plunge them into second division until 1925.

1929

A'S WORLD CHAMPS! STOCKS CRASH!

AT LEAST OUR STOCK IS UP!

.365

A's 15-year pennant drought ends when club wins 104 games, plus World Series over Chicago Cubs in five. Al Simmons (.365) leads A's in homers with 34 and AL in RBIs (157). Jimmie Foxx hits 33 homers, while George Earnshaw wins 24 and Lefty Grove 20, with a league-leading 2.81 ERA.

1950

SOME GUYS ONLY HAVE BIG SHOES TO FILL!

MACK

Mack's 50-year managerial tenure, one in which he won nine AL flags and five World Series, ends at age 87. Former A's third baseman Jimmy Dykes replaces him. (Without a pennant since '31, A's landed in second division 16 times in 19 seasons between 1931 and 1950, 10 of them in AL cellar.)

The financially strapped A's move to Kansas City as Mack's sons, Earle and Roy, sell franchise to Arnold Johnson and midwestern group. Lou Boudreau becomes KC skipper, and club finishes sixth, its highest windup in what will be 13 seasons in Kansas City.

The controversial Charles O. Finley purchases A's from Johnson's estate and begins a seven-season stay in KC that features his becoming embroiled with fans, media, managers, players, and baseball hierarchy.

Finley, his bridges burned behind him, abandons Kansas City for Oakland, where his club finishes sixth, winning 82 games, the most by an A's club since 1948. Reggie Jackson hits 29 homers, while Blue Moon Odom wins 16 and Jim (Catfish) Hunter 13.

Jackson socks career-high 47 homers, and revived A's land second in AL West in first saison of divisional play. Third baseman Sal Bando hits 31 homers, while righty Chuck Dobson and Odom each win 15. Hunter wins 12, and righty reliever Rollie Fingers chalks up a dozen saves.

The first of three straight pennants and World Series triumphs occurs when A's win West by 5½, defeat Detroit for AL flag, and upset Cincinnati in seven-game World Series. Hunter wins 21 and lefty Ken Holtzman 19, and Fingers has 21 saves.

Oakland again wins it all: division, flag, and seven-game World Series victory over New York Mets. Williams, in constant conflict with Finley, resigns after Series. Jackson, the MVP, leads AL with 32 homers and 117 RBIs. Holtzman and Hunter each win 21 and Blue chalks up 20.

The A's, under Dick Williams, begin five-season run of success, as they win AL West by 16 games but bow to Baltimore in pennant playoff. Lefty Vida Blue, in his first full season, wins 25 and leads AL with 1.82 ERA. He wins both Cy Young and MVP laurels. Hunter wins 21, and Jackson hits 32 homers.

Alvin Dark leads A's to division, flag, and five-game Series win over Los Angeles Dodgers. Hunter captures Cy Young with 25–12 season and league-leading 2.49 ERA but during winter gains free agency and signs with Yankees.

A's win West by seven but are upset by Boston in AL pennant playoff. Jackson's 36 homers paces AL, and, like Hunter, he becomes free agent and joins Yankees. Blue (22–11) is A's top winner, and Holtzman adds 18, while Fingers registers two dozen saves.

Chuck Tanner replaces Dark as manager but is gone when A's finish 2½ games behind KC Royals in AL West. Bando paces club with 27 homers. Joe Rudi leads in RBIs with 94. Blue (18–13) and Mike Torrez (16–12) lead staff, to which Fingers contributes 20 saves.

A's plunge into AL West cellar, losing 98 games. Third baseman Wayne Gross leads club with 22 home runs. Mitchell Page hits 21. Blue (14–19) leads staff in wins. Righty Doc Medich goes 10–6 and is lone hurler to finish above .500.

Club lands sixth, as Page's .285 average and 17 homers lead A's offense. Club's .245 batting average is lowest in American League. Lefty John Henry Johnson (11–10) is top moundsman. Righty Pete Broberg follows him with 10–12 mark. Righty Elias Sosa is 8–2 in relief with 14 saves.

Billy Martin becomes manager and raises A's from last to second in AL West. Sophomore outfielder Rickey Henderson bats .303 and begins string of seven straight stolen-base titles when he swipes 100. Right fielder Tony Armas hits 35 homers, and righty Mike Norris wins 22.

Finley finally sells franchise in November 1980, and the Oakland purchasers celebrate with an AL West title in strike-shortened season. A's lose pennant playoff to Yankees, but they get 22 homers from Armas and 14 wins from righty Steve McCatty, who leads AL with 2.32 ERA.

A's dip to fifth, and their 94 losses cost Martin his job, as the pitching sours, compiling a 4.54 ERA. Righty Matt Keough wins 11 but loses 18 and leads the league in defeats. Armas clouts 28 homers, and Henderson's 130 steals are a one-season major-league record.

Pitching continues to hobble Oakland, as rookie righty Chris Codiroli is the A's top winner with 12 victories. Second baseman Dave Lopes and center fielder Dwayne Murphy share the club homer lead with 17, while third baseman Carney Lansford bats .308.

The A's, with Tony LaRussa taking over as manager in July, finish fourth. DH Dave Kingman hits 35 homers, and outfielder Jose Canseco, AL's Rookie award winner, cracks 33. Lefty Curt Young (13–9) paces the staff, and righty Jay Howell leads relievers with 16 saves.

Oakland, with first baseman Mark McGwire hitting a rookie-record 49 home runs, which earn him Rookie of the Year honors, finishes third with .500 record. Righty Dave Stewart goes 20–13, Young 13–7. The bullpen shines, as Howell and righty Dennis Eckersley each save 16.

LaRussa leads A's to 104 wins and AL pennant. Though upset by Dodgers in World Series, loss doesn't detract from Canseco's MVP year, which includes 42 homers and 124 RBIs. Stewart wins 21, and Eckersley sets club mark with 45 saves.

Another pennant, plus a four-straight sweep of the neighboring San Francisco Giants in an earthquake-interrupted World Series. Stewart again wins 21, while righties Mike Moore and Storm Davis each win 19. Eckersley saves 33 and McGwire paces club with 33 homers.

A third AL pennant is soiled when Cincinnati sweeps A's in four straight in World Series. Veteran righty Bob Welch (27–6) wins Cy Young Award. Stewart (22–11) wins 20 for fourth straight year. Eckersley saves 48 to break his club mark. Henderson is AL's MVP with .325 average, 28 homers, and league-leading 65 stolen bases. In 1991 he passes Lou Brock as the all-time base stealing champ.

Seattle Mariners

1984 First baseman Alvin Davis, with 27 homers and 116 RBIs, is AL's Rookie of the Year, as Mariners reach sixth place. Lefty DH Ken Phelps hits 24 homers, and rookie southpaw Mark Langston goes 17–10 to lead club's staff. Righty Jim Beattie follows with 12–16 log.

1977 HOME, SWEET DOME!

The AL expands to 14 clubs, and the Mariners are established and move into the Kingdome, a 58,000-seat indoor arena. Despite sixth-place finish, club draws 1,338,511 in maiden season. Outfielder Leroy Stanton hits 27 homers, and Glenn Abbott (12–13) leads staff.

1982 THROW A SPITTER? LOAD UP A BASEBALL? —WHO, ME?

Mariners win 76 and land fourth in AL West. Designated hitter Richie Zisk leads club with 21 homers, one more than right fielder Al Cowens. Reliever Bill Caudill is most productive hurler with 12 wins and 26 saves. Veteran Gaylord Perry wins career victory No. 300.

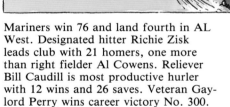

1983

A team batting average of .240, lowest in AL, plunges Mariners back into basement, as they lose 102. Left fielder Steve Henderson's .294 average is club's best. Left-hander Matt Young (11–15) has the most wins, and no Seattle pitcher has a winning record.

1985 STORMIN' GORMAN!

Another sixth-place landing, as veteran DH Gorman Thomas leads squad with 32 homers. Left fielder Phil Bradley bats .300 and hits 26 homers. Righty Mike Moore heads staff with 17–10 record, while Langston slips to 7–14.

Seattle sinks to cellar despite 27 homers and 107 RBIs from third baseman Jim Presley. Right fielder Danny Tartabull follows with 25 homers and 96 RBIs. Langston (12–14) is staff's big winner. Righty Mike Morgan (11–17) leads AL in losses.

Veteran manager Dick Williams steers club to record 78 wins and fourth place in AL West. Davis hits 29 homers and drives in 100. Phelps pops 27 homers and Presley 24. Langston (19–13) is tops, with lefty Lee Guetterman going 11–4.

Mariners, unable to sustain 1987 output, topple back into cellar with 93 defeats. Langston (15–11) is only starter with winning mark. Rookie righty Mike Schooler debuts as reliever with 15 saves. Davis leads club with .295 average and adds 18 homers and 69 RBIs.

Jim Lefebvre debuts as Seattle skipper, and club rises to sixth. Davis's .305 average leads team, as do his 95 RBIs. DH Jeffrey Leonard paces club with 24 homers. Right-hander Scott Bankhead, replacing departed Langston, wins 14. Schooler ups saves to 33.

Mariners advance to fifth, and 6'10" lefty Randy Johnson, tallest player in major-league history, wins 14, including first no-hitter by a Mariner. Righty Erik Hanson leads staff with 18 wins, and Schooler saves 30. Outfielder Ken Griffey, Jr., who is joined by 40-year-old dad on August 31—another major-league first—bats .300 with 22 homers.

Texas Rangers

1974

Martin's "magic" lifts Rangers to 84 wins and second place in AL West. First baseman Mike Hargrove bats .323 and is AL's Rookie of the Year. Burroughs is its MVP, with .301 average, 25 homers, and league-leading 118 RBIs. Right-hander Ferguson Jenkins goes 25–12.

ABRACADABRA!

1972

100 LOSSES! THAT'S IT! I'M TURNING IN MY BADGE!

The American League shifts its Washington franchise to the Dallas–Ft. Worth area, and the Senators are renamed the Rangers. Manager Ted Williams's club loses 100 games, and ends up in sixth, and he resigns.

1973

BURROUGHS WILL HELP TEXAS BURROW OUT OF THE CELLAR!

POW!

Rangers lose club-high 105 and retain cellar. Right-hander Jim Bibby (9–10) is biggest winner. Outfielder Jeff Burroughs hits 30 homers and drives in 85. Billy Martin's being named manager in September promises brighter future.

1975

BILLY, DON'T YOU THINK THAT YOU'VE STAYED TOO LONG WITH THAT PITCHER?

BILLY, MAYBE YOU SHOULD SHIFT THE OUTFIELDERS A WEE BIT...

Rangers drop to third, and Martin, blaming front-office interference, is dropped July 21. Burroughs hits 29 homers and has 94 RBIs. Shortstop Toby Harrah hits 20 homers, and Hargrove bats .303. Jenkins (17–18) is top winner, while Gaylord Perry goes 12–8.

1985

♪ ...EACH DAY IS VALENTINE'S DAY... ♪

Bobby Valentine named manager in May but can't avert cellar finish via 99 losses. First baseman Pete O'Brien leads club with 22 homers and 92 RBIs. Pitching is problem. Charlie Hough (14–16) is staff's best. Righty Greg Harris wins five and saves 11 out of pen.

Valentine, à la Martin, juices Rangers to second place. Outfielder Pete Incaviglia hits club-high 30 homers, while designated hitter Larry Parrish hits 28. Hough (17–10) is mound ace, and righty Bobby Witt goes 11–9. Harris wins 10, saves 20 as reliever.

Rangers finish tied for sixth with Angels. Soph outfielder Ruben Sierra hits 30 homers and leads squad with 109 RBIs. Parrish clouts 32 and drives in 100. Despite Hough's 18–13 showing, pitching is a minus, although reliever Dale Mohorcic produces 16 saves.

Rangers again land sixth despite 23 homers from Sierra and 22 from Incaviglia. Right-hander Jeff Russell (10–9) is only pitcher above .500. Hough (15–16) is top winner. Lefty reliever Mitch Williams, dealt to Cubs during following winter, has 18 saves.

Free agent Nolan Ryan leads staff with 16 wins and leads AL with 301 strikeouts, one of which is career No. 5,000. Club finishes fourth, as Russell saves 38. Sierra's 119 RBIs lead league, and his 29 homers lead ballclub.

Rangers land third, and Ryan wins 13, including his 300th lifetime, and adds record sixth no-hitter (In 1991 he pitched his seventh). Witt (17–10) is top winner. Incaviglia paces club with 24 homers. Rafael Palmero bats .319, while switch-hitting Jack Daugherty bats .300.

Toronto Blue Jays

1983

The Jays go 89–73 and land fourth in AL East. Stieb (17–12) is mound ace. Clancy goes 15–11. Righty Randy Moffitt chalks up 10 saves. Outfielder Jesse Barfield and Upshaw each hit 27 home runs. Outfielder Barry Bonnell paces hitters with .318 average.

1977

GOOD DAY, EH?

The American League moves to Canada, establishing an expansion franchise in Toronto. Club, called the Blue Jays, loses 107 and finishes last in AL East. Dave Lemanczyk (13–16) is club's top winner. Ron Fairly leads team with 19 homers, and Bob Bailor hits .310.

1978

WOW! 1.2 MILLION! THAT'S A LOT OF PEOPLE TO FIT IN A CELLAR!

Another basement windup, via 102 losses, but 1.2 million fans show support in Toronto. Jim Clancy (10–12) is top winner, and reliever Victor Cruz saves nine. John Mayberry leads roster with 22 homers, and veteran DH Rico Carty tops hitters with .284 average.

1982

... CAN'T WE SHARE?

After five straight cellar finishes, Jays, under manager Bobby Cox, win 78 and tie for sixth place with Indians. Righty Dave Stieb (17–14) and Clancy (16–14) are staff's best. Righty Dale Murray paces pen with 11 saves. First baseman Willie Upshaw hits 21 homers.

1984

NEXT STOP, THE TOP!

Toronto advances to second place, as outfielder George Bell hits 26 homers and infielder Rance Mulliniks bats .324. Veteran righty Doyle Alexander tops pitchers with 17 wins, while Stieb goes 16–8. Righty reliever Roy Lee Jackson and lefty Jimmy Key prop pen with 10 saves apiece.

The Jays win 99 and AL East, but pennant dream vanishes via loss to Kansas City in playoff. Alexander again is tops, with 17–10 record, and Key, now a starter, goes 14–6. Tom Henke, promoted in July, chalks up 13 saves. Bell's 28 homers are most on squad.

Jays tie with Milwaukee for third place, as Stieb goes 16–8 and Henke posts 25 saves. First baseman Fred McGriff hits 34 homers, 10 more than Bell, who leads club with 97 RBIs. Mulliniks tops club with .300 average, and third baseman Kelly Gruber knocks in 81 runs.

Coach Cito Gaston named manager in May, and Jays respond with 89 wins and East title. In June club moves into 51,000-seat Skydome. Stieb leads staff with 17–8 mark, while Henke chalks up 20 saves. McGriff leads AL with 36 homers. Season dulled by pennant loss to Oakland.

Jays finish second but draw major-league-high 3,885,284 fans to Skydome. McGriff bats .300 and leads club with 35 homers, four more than Gruber. Stieb goes 18–6, plus a no-hitter. Key and fellow lefty Bud Black each win 13, and Henke saves 32 games.

Following fourth-place finish in 1986, Jays rebound to second place in AL East. Key leads staff with 17 wins, while Clancy wins 15 and Stieb 13. Henke saves 34. Bell hits 47 homers and is AL's MVP because of .308 average and league-leading 134 RBIs.

Atlanta Braves

1957 Braves shed "bridesmaid" role when they win flag and upset New York Yankees in seven-game World Series. Spahn, Cy Young winner, leads league with 21 wins. Righty Lew Burdette wins 17, plus three in Series. Outfielder Henry Aaron leads NL with 44 homers and 132 RBIs and is MPV.

...AND WE FINALLY CAUGHT THE BOUQUET!

1957 CHAMPS

1876 *GEORGE! BY JOVE! GOOD SHOW! HAVE A SPOT OF TEA!*

Boston begins its 76-year tenure in the newly formed National League. The club finishes fourth in the eight-team group. British-born Harry Wright and his brother, George, each of whom will be Hall of Famers, serve as manager and shortstop, respectively.

1914 *"RIGHT" MAKES MIGHT!*

A series of second-division finishes terminates when Boston, known as the Braves, win pennant by 10½ games. They wipe out powerful Philadelphia A's in four straight in World Series. Righties Dick Rudolph (27–10) and Bill James (26–7) are mound stars.

1948 *WELL, WE'VE USED SPAHN AND SAIN... ...ANYBODY HEARD THE WEATHER REPORT??*

The Braves end 34-year flag drought when they win NL by 6½ games. Right-hander Johnny Sain (24–15) and lefty Warren Spahn (15–12) prompt famed ditty "Spahn and Sain and a day of rain." Dream ends when Cleveland defeats Braves in six-game World Series.

1953 *WE'RE THE BRAVES THAT'LL MAKE MILWAUKEE FAMOUS!*

Less than a month before season opener, the Braves abandon Boston for Milwaukee in a historic franchise shift. The move pays dividends, as club, with Spahn winning 23 and third baseman Eddie Mathews leading NL with 47 homers, rises to second place.

1958 *IT'S TOUGH TO BE BRAVE IN DEFEAT!*

Another NL flag, but Braves drop Series to Yankees in seven games. Spahn's 22 wins lead NL, while Burdette posts 20. Club gets punch from Mathews's 31 homers and Aaron's 30. Outfielder Wes Covington chips in with .330 average, plus 24 home runs.

1966 *44 BY NUMBER 44!*

The Braves, down at the gate and in the standings, desert Milwaukee for Atlanta, but move finds them fifth in 10-club NL. Aaron, with 44 homers and 127 RBIs, leads league, while catcher Joe Torre bats .315 with 36 homers and 101 RBIs. Right-handers Tony Cloninger and Ken Johnson each win 14.

1969

NL goes to divisional play, and Braves surprise by winning NL West with 93 victories. Pennant, however, is lost to Mets. Aaron, with .300 average, 44 homers and 97 RBIs, continues to be Braves' big bopper. Phil Niekro wins 23, and reliever Cecil Upshaw saves 27.

1970

Braves sag to fifth despite Rico Carty's league-leading .366 average. Aaron celebrates 3,000th career base hit. Right-hander Pat Jarvis (16–16) is staff's top winner. First baseman Orlando Cepeda, acquired from St. Louis for Torre, bats .305 with 34 homers and 111 RBIs.

1971

Club lands third in NL West, as Aaron hits 47 homers, one of which is his 600th career four-bagger. Catcher Earl Williams, Rookie of the Year, hits 33 homers and has 87 RBIs. Niekro (15–14) is top pitcher, while Upshaw contributes 17 saves.

1973

Braves sink to fifth, despite Dave Johnson (43), Darrell Evans (41), and Aaron (40) setting home-run record for number of players on one team hitting 40 or more in a season. Niekro wins 13, including no-hitter over Padres, but staff's 4.25 ERA is league's highest.

1975

Braves lose 94 and slide to fifth. Evans leads club with 22 homers, and outfielder Dusty Baker hits 19. Morton (17–16) paces staff in victories. Niekro is 15–15, and no other Atlanta hurler has more than seven wins.

1976

TV magnate Ted Turner purchases club and makes big splash by signing free agent Andy Messersmith to $1 million contract. Braves land at bottom of NL West, as Messersmith goes 11–11. Niekro (17–11) is staff's top winner. Left fielder Jimmy Wynn bats .207 but leads club with 17 home runs.

1974

Aaron ties Babe Ruth's homer record on Opening Day, and on April 8, at Atlanta, hits record-setting 715th homer. Club finishes third, and left fielder Ralph Garr's .353 average is best in NL. Aaron, in final season as a Brave, hits 20 homers. Niekro goes 20–13, while righties Carl Morton and Buzz Capra each win 16.

MVP! MVP!

1983
Murphy wins second consecutive MVP with 36 homers and league-leading 121 RBIs, but Braves finish second to Dodgers by three games. Horner and lefty-hitting first baseman Chris Chambliss each hit 20 homers. Rookie righty Craig McMurtry and righty Pascual Perez each win 15, and righty reliever Steve Bedrosian chalks up 19 saves.

1977

HEY! WE'RE LOSIN' ANYWAY—WHY SHOULD I PAY EXTRA FOR A MANAGER?!?

Braves, with 101 losses, renew cellar lease. Turner manages club for one game during 17-game losing streak then Commissioner Bowie Kuhn prohibits him. Niekro wins 16, but Braves' staff's 4.85 ERA is highest in NL. Jeff Burroughs hits career-high 41 homers.

1978

YOU GUYS WANT THE BRAVES? THEY LIVE IN THE BASEMENT!

NL WEST

Another cellar windup is tempered by arrival of Dale Murphy and Bob Horner. Murphy hits 23 homers. Horner also hits 23 and is NL's Rookie of the Year. Niekro (19–18) and rookie Larry McWilliams (9–3) are only full-time starters to post winning records.

1979

NIEKRO, I'M SURE YOU'VE HAD YOUR PHIL OF LOSING!

Niekro wins 21, while Horner belies Braves' fourth-straight cellar finish by hitting 33 homers and driving in 98 runs. Outfielder Gary Matthews hits 27 with 90 RBIs, while Murphy contributes 21 homers. Atlanta staff's 4.18 ERA is worst in NL.

1980

Braves climb to fourth, one game over .500, as Horner bangs 35 homers, and Murphy, shifting to outfield, hits 33. Atlanta's pitching continues to stagger. Niekro (15–18) is top producer. Righty Doyle Alexander goes 14–11, and righty reliever Rick Camp produces career-high 22 saves.

1981

THAT'S IT! I'M STRIKIN' OUT...FOR ANOTHER COUNTRY!

COX

Braves CLUBHOUSE

When Braves slide back to fifth in strike-marred season, manager Bobby Cox opts for contract in Toronto. Horner leads club with 15 homers, two more than Murphy. Ageless Gaylord Perry wins eight, as does righty Rick Mahler. Camp goes 9–3 with 17 saves.

1982

MY BOYS ARE SETTING A TORREID PACE!

Joe Torre takes Braves' job and leads club to divisional crown although club is eliminated by St. Louis in pennant playoff. Braves set record by winning first 13 games. Murphy, with 36 homers and league-leading 109 RBIs, is NL's MVP. Niekro wins 17, and reliever Gene Garber saves 30.

Another second-place finish costs Torre his job. Murphy's 36 homers lead NL, while Perez (14–8) and Mahler (13–10) pace the pitching staff. Veteran right-hander Donnie Moore leads bullpen brigade with 16 saves.

Eddie Haas's career as skipper ends while Braves are en route to 96 losses and fifth place in NL West. Mahler, (17–15) is only winning starter, but reliever Bruce Sutter saves 23. Murphy's 37 homers lead league, and Horner, now a first baseman, hits 27.

Chuck Tanner takes over as manager, and Braves drop into NL West basement. Garber saves 24, but Mahler, the top winner, goes 14–18. Murphy leads club with 29 home runs, and Horner has 27, four of which come against Montreal on July 6.

The pitching goes south, as staff's 4.63 ERA is highest in NL. A good offense enables Braves to reach fifth place. Murphy whacks 44 homers and drives in 105 runners. Lefty Zane Smith wins 15 and is the only Braves' hurler with a winning record.

Tanner is dismissed in May, and Braves lose 106 and sink into NL West cellar. Murphy, despite a .226 average, hits 24 home runs and leads squad with 77 RBIs. Lefty Paul Assenmacher, out of the pen, goes 8–7 and is only pitcher above .500.

Braves continue to occupy basement, and their .234 batting mark is lowest in league. Left fielder Lonnie Smith hits .315 and leads club with 21 homers, one more than Murphy. Lefty Tom Glavine goes 14–8, while righty John Smoltz, the NL starter in the All-Star Game, finishes at 12–11.

Atlanta renews basement slot, as the pitchers' 4.58 ERA is highest in majors. Smoltz (14–11) and Glavine (10–12) are club's only hurlers to win in double figures. Ron Gant leads club with 32 homers, while Rookie of the Year Dave Justice hits 28. Murphy's Atlanta career ends when he goes to Phillies in late-season deal.

Chicago Cubs

1908

With famed Tinker-Evers-Chance double-play combination fueling their efforts, Cubs win pennant by one game over New York Giants. Three Finger Brown and fellow right-hander Orval Overall each win two games in World Series, and the club defeats Detroit in five games. It's the last World Series the Cubs have won.

1876

THIS SHOULD HELP SALES!

Chicago is the only club to play continuously in the same city since formation of the NL in 1876. With manager/pitcher Albert G. Spalding, who later founded famed sporting-goods firm, the team wins 52 of 66 games played and cops NL's first pennant.

1906

WHO NEEDS FOUR FINGERS!?!

Hall of Fame right-hander Mordecai (Three Finger) Brown has the first of his six straight 20-win seasons. Chicago wins NL pennant with all-time major-league record of 116 wins, but team is upset in World Series by "Hitless Wonder" Chicago White Sox.

1907

ALRIGHT, ALRIGHT! SINCE YOU INSIST ON CARRYING TEDDY BEARS...

Chicago club formally adopts name "Cubs." They again win pennant, but this time they capture World Series, defeating Detroit in four straight after clubs play 3–3 tie in Series' opener.

1916

CHEER UP, GUYS, IT WON'T BE LONG BEFORE WE'RE CHAMPS AGAIN!

Cubs move into Weeghman Park (now known as Wrigley Field), a park that housed the ill-fated Federal League team. Cubs, however, can't celebrate because their fifth-place finish is club's lowest in 13 years.

1918

HIPPO, YOU DID A WHALE OF A JOB!

Left-hander Jim (Hippo) Vaughn wins league-high 22 games. Cubs win National League flag by 10½ games over New York Giants, but L'il Bears drop World Series to Boston Red Sox in six games.

1929

POW!

I NEVER PLAYED BUT I COULDA PLAYED BETTER THAN THIS!

Second baseman Rogers Hornsby and center fielder Hack Wilson each sock 39 homers. Joe McCarthy, who never played in majors, skippers Cubs to National League pennant. His club loses Series to Philadelphia A's in five after blowing 8–0 lead in seventh inning of Game 4.

Roly-poly outfielder Wilson sets National League home-run record (56) and major league RBI record (190). Cubs, despite 90 wins, finish second to St. Louis Cardinals in pennant chase.

First baseman Charlie Grimm replaces Rogers Hornsby as manager in mid-season. With right-hander Lon Warneke winning 22 games, Cubs win flag by four over Pittsburgh but are bombed in four straight by New York Yankees in World Series.

Warneke and fellow righty Bill Lee each win 20. Fueled by their 21-game winning streak in September, Cubs win National League pennant, but the season is spoiled by six-game World Series loss to Detroit.

First baseman Phil Cavarretta's .355 batting average leads National League. With Charlie Grimm again as skipper, Cubs win pennant over St. Louis but drop seven-game World Series to Detroit.

Cubs acquire home-run slugger Ralph Kiner from Pittsburgh in 10-player trade, with Cubs yielding six players, plus $150,000. Kiner's 28 homers for his new club don't prevent Cubs' seventh-place finish.

On May 12 right-handed curveballer Sam Jones becomes first black pitcher to hurl a no-hitter. He defeats Pittsburgh 4–0, despite walking seven in game at Wrigley Field.

Hall of Fame catcher Gabby Hartnett replaces Charlie Grimm as manager in midseason. He hits late-season home run that virtually assures Cubs the National League pennant over Pittsburgh. But once again Cubbies are buried in four in a row by Yankees in World Series.

1958

Hall of Famer Ernie Banks leads National League in homers (47) and RBIs (129) and wins MVP award. This is the first time the prize has ever gone to a player on a club with a losing record. Fifth-place Cubs finish 10 games

LET'S PLAY TWO!

1959

YOU CAN BANK ON ME!

MVP

Ernie Banks leads National League with 143 RBIs and repeats as MVP. Cubs, playing six games below .500, finish in a fifth-place tie with Cincinnati.

1960

I GUESS I HANDLED THE CARDS PRETTY WELL!

Right-hander Don Cardwell, acquired from the Phillies on May 13, celebrates his arrival at Wrigley Field by no-hitting St. Louis, 4–0. This is his first Chicago start, two days after the trade.

1966

WELL, AT LEAST THERE'S NO PLACE TO GO BUT UP!

Leo Durocher, who earlier managed Dodgers and Giants to NL pennants, ends 11-year retirement as major-league skipper by accepting job as Cubs' manager. After announcing his team isn't an eighth-place club, his players prove it — by finishing 10th and last in NL.

1967

Right-hander Ferguson Jenkins registers the first of his six straight 20-victory seasons. Cubs rebound to third place.

1969

AMAZIN!!

WHOOSH!

Cubs, despite owning 9½-game lead in mid-August, are overwhelmed by New York Mets' second-half spurt. They lose National League East by eight games despite 21 wins from Jenkins and 20 from fellow right-hander Bill Hands.

1971

WELL, HARD WORK DOES HAVE IT'S REWARDS!

CY

Jenkins leads National League in victories (24) and innings pitched (325) and is named Cy Young Award winner. Cubs finish third in National League East, tied with New York Mets.

Rookie right-hander Burt Hooton, master of the knuckle-curve, pitches 4–0 no-hitter over Philadelphia, April 16, at Wrigley Field. Cubs finish second, 11 games behind Pittsburgh. Durocher is dismissed as manager at All-Star break.

Right-hander Bruce Sutter, famed for his split-fingered fastball, leads majors with 37 saves. Despite Cubs' fifth-place finish in National League East, Sutter is rewarded with National League's Cy Young Award.

Right-hander Rick Sutcliffe, obtained from Cleveland in June, goes 16–1 to lead Cubs to National League East title and himself to Cy Young prize. But L'il Bears lose best-of-five pennant playoff to San Diego.

Outfielder Andre Dawson, formerly a star for Montreal, signs free-agent contract with Cubs. He not only wins National League homer (49) and RBI (137) titles but is league's MVP as well.

Historic Wrigley Field, with its famed ivy-covered outfield walls, the oldest park in the National League, is given a brand-new look: Lights are installed and night ball is played.

Manager Don Zimmer, with second baseman Ryne Sandberg hitting 30 homers and lefty reliever Mitch Williams adding 36 saves, leads Cubs to 93 wins and National League East title. But club is downed by San Francisco Giants in five-game pennant playoff.

Wrigley Field hosts All-Star game in July. Ryne Sandberg, along with celebrating personal high in homers (40), sets major-league record for errorless games by a second baseman (123) and record of errorless chances (582).

Cincinnati Reds

Lefty Johnny Vander Meer becomes only pitcher in major-league history to toss successive no-hitters, June 11 vs. Boston and June 15 vs. Brooklyn. Manager Bill McKechnie guides Reds to fourth-place finish.

1938

JUST SAY "NO-NO"!

JUNE 15TH VS. BROOKLYN

JUNE 11TH VS. BOSTON

1869 HARRY, IF WE'RE THE FIRST PRO TEAM—WHO ARE **WE** GONNA PLAY?

The Cincinnati Red Stockings become baseball's first all-professional team. Hall of Famer Harry Wright, with a reported salary of $1,200, is manager, and his younger brother, George, also a Hall-of-Famer-to-be, plays shortstop.

1876 LET'S HEAR IT, BOYS!... HIP-HIP...AWW FORGET IT!

Cincinnati is granted a franchise in newly formed National League. Celebrations are limited because club finishes in cellar, winning only 9 and losing 56.

1905 ..HOW ABOUT THE "CY" SEYMOUR AWARD... HMMM.... HAS A NICE RING TO IT!

Outfielder Cy Seymour's .377 batting average, still a one-season high for a Reds' player, wins National League batting crown. Club winds up in fifth place.

1919 .321 I'M IN A ROUSH TO WIN!

Outfielder Edd Roush, future Hall of Famer, leads Reds to first pennant and a World Series win over Chicago. He leads league with .321 average, and Reds finish nine games ahead of the New York Giants.

1935 MR. MacPHAIL, YOU FORGOT TO SWITCH ON THE LIGHTS! BONK!

1935—General manager Larry MacPhail, one of game's foremost promoters, introduces night baseball to the major leagues. On May 24, at Cincinnati's Crosley Field, the Reds beat Philadelphia, 2–1.

1939

Right-hander Bucky Walters wins 27 games and is the National League's MVP. Reds' first NL flag in 20 years becomes slightly tattered when New York Yankees sweep World Series in four straight.

First baseman Frank McCormick is National League's MVP. Walters (22–10) and right-hander Paul Derringer (20–12) each win two games in seven-game World Series win over Detroit Tigers.

Sidearming right-hander Ewell Blackwell wins 22. He hurls no-hitter over Boston June 18 and misses a second on a ninth-inning hit vs. Brooklyn Dodgers in his next start.

Manager Fred Hutchinson leads Reds to National League flag. Robinson is National League's MVP, but Cincinnati bows to New York Yankees in a five-game World Series.

Pete Rose, whose enthusiasm earns him nickname "Charlie Hustle," bursts on the scene and is named National League's Rookie of the Year.

Catcher Johnny Bench, who played in 26 games in 1967, launches his Hall of Fame career by winning Rookie of the Year honors. He revolutionizes the art of catching with his defense and potent throwing arm.

Freshman manager Sparky Anderson leads Reds to National League pennant. In his eight seasons at Reds' helm, they will win five Western Division titles, four pennants, and two World Series as the famed "Big Red Machine."

Outfielder Frank Robinson hits 38 home runs, tying a record for a rookie. He helps Reds tie major-league record for homers by a club (221), as Cincy finishes third, two games behind Brooklyn.

Reds slide to fourth win 79–83 record, the worst they'll have under Sparky Anderson. A postseason deal that brings Joe Morgan from Houston sets the stage for club's future successes.

Bench is again the National League's MVP. Reds win National League West and defeat Pittsburgh in five-game playoff on a ninth-inning wild pitch. They lose World Series to Oakland in seven games.

Rose wins National League batting title for third time and is also National League's MVP. Cincy wins West, only to bow to New York Mets in five-game pennant playoff.

Second baseman Morgan wins first of two successive MVP awards. Mighty Reds crown season by winning seven-game World Series from Boston Red Sox.

Reds continue to roll, winning West title and National League pennant with three-game sweep of Philadelphia. They also sweep New York Yankees, four in a row, in the World Series.

Outfielder George Foster hits team-record 52 home runs and is named National League's MVP, but Reds finish second, 10 games behind the Dodgers.

Rose ties National League record by hitting safely in 44 consecutive games. Cincinnati again trails Los Angeles Dodgers in Western Division race, landing 2½ games behind.

Rose, a free agent, signs with Phillies. John McNamara replaces Sparky Anderson as Reds' skipper, leading club to Western Division title before bowing to Pittsburgh in pennant playoff.

Right-hander Tom Seaver, whom Reds obtained in 1977 and who no-hitted St. Louis the following year, becomes only the fifth pitcher in history to record 3,000 career strikeouts.

Rose comes home after playing five years with Phillies and part of 1984 season with Montreal. He is named Reds' manager upon his arrival on August 16.

Lefty Tom Browning, who won 20 games as rookie in 1985, authors perfect game over Dodgers on September 16. Reds still finish seven behind Los Angeles in divisional race.

Johnny Bench is voted into Hall of Fame on first ballot. Commissioner Bart Giamatti bans Pete Rose in an August 24 decision that makes huge headlines and generates speculation over Pete's Hall of Fame chances in 1992.

Longtime Yankees player and manager Lou Piniella signs contract to skipper Reds. Following fast start, Cincy wins Western Division and NL pennant over Pittsburgh. (For the first time in history one team leads the NL wire to wire.) In a major upset, they sweep Oakland in the World Series.

Rose, as player-manager, breaks Ty Cobb's all-time base-hit record when he collects hit No. 4,192 on September 11 vs. San Diego Padres.

Houston Astros

1965

Club is renamed Astros when it moves into 51,000-seat Astrodome, baseball's first indoor park. The team loses club-record 97 games, finishing ninth. Center fielder Jimmy Wynn leads squad with 22 homers, while right fielder Rusty Staub and second baseman Joe Morgan each hit 14. Farrell's 11 wins lead the staff.

WYNN-ING IN THE 'DOME!

YOUNG GUNS!

The NL expands to 10 clubs, and the Houston Colt .45s are born. They surprise everyone by finishing eighth, with a 64–96 record. Roman Mejias leads club with .286 average, 24 homers, and 76 RBIs. Bob Bruce and Dick Farrell each win 10 games.

ANOTHER HAT TRICK FROM "HARRY THE HAT"!

Astros reach .500 for the first time, finishing fifth with 81–81 record under manager Harry Walker. Don Wilson authors second no-hitter, this one vs. Cincinnati. Larry Dierker (20–13) is Houston's first 20-game winner. Jimmy Wynn leads club with 33 home runs.

DUROCHER, YOU'RE AN ASTRO-NUT!

Leo Durocher becomes manager in August, and club wins 84 games to finish second in NL West. Righties Don Wilson and Larry Dierker lead mound corps with 15 victories each. First baseman Lee May is big bopper with 29 homers and 98 RBIs.

WE'RE THE BEST! —IN THE WEST, ANYWAY...

1980 CHAMPS NL WEST

Astros, after several so-so seasons, win NL West with 93 victories under manager Bill Virdon. But NL flag is lost in best-of-five playoff vs. Phillies. Right-hander Joe Niekro wins 20. Free-agent righty Nolan Ryan wins 11. Outfielder Cesar Cedeno leads club with .309 average.

Astros win second half of strike-marred season but lose West title to Dodgers. Don Sutton and Ryan each win 11, one of which is Ryan's fifth career no-hitter. Third baseman Art Howe's .296 average is club high, while Jose Cruz paces roster with 13 homers and 55 RBIs.

Houston dips to fifth in AL West. Joe Niekro (17–12) leads staff while Ryan goes 16–12 and Sutton 13–8. Lack of offense stalls attack, as Ray Knight's .294 average is team's tops. Second baseman Phil Garner leads club with 13 homers and 83 RBIs.

Houston ties Braves for second, and Niekro is again staff leader with 16 wins. Lefty Bob Knepper goes 15–10, and Ryan wins a dozen. Cruz paces offense with .312 average, 12 homers, and 95 RBIs. First baseman Enos Cabell bats .310.

Astros tie Padres for third place. Right-hander Mike Scott is big winner with 18. Knepper goes 15–13 and Ryan 10½–12. Rookie first baseman Glenn Davis leads club with 20 home runs, and Cruz's .300 average tops hitters.

Astros advance to third, as Cruz leads charge with .318 average. Shortstop Dickie Thon hits 20 home runs. Niekro is top winner with 15. Ryan wins 14 and breaks Walter Johnson's all-time career strikeout record when he chalks up No. 3,509 vs. Montreal.

1986

Houston wins division with club-record 96 victories but loses NL flag playoff with Mets in six games. Scott, Cy Young Award winner, chalks up 18 wins, and his 2.22 ERA is NL's best. Davis hits 31 homers and drives in 101.

1987

27 ASTRO-MOONSHOTS!

Club slides to third despite 16 wins from Scotr and Ryan's league-leading 2.76 ERA. Davis paces Houston with 27 homers and 93 RBIs. Outfielder Kevin Bass contributes 19 home runs, and second baseman Bill Doran hits 16.

1988

"DAVE"—IT RHYMES WITH "SAVE"!

Astros dip to fifth despite 82–80 record. Davis pops 30 home runs and drives home 99 runners. Bass, with 14, is only other Astro to homer in double figures. Scott and Knepper lead staff with 14 wins each. Righty reliever Dave Smith saves 27.

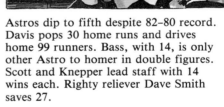

1989

HOWE GOOD A MANAGER AM I?

Rookie manager Art Howe boosts Astros to third, getting 20 victories from Scott. Veteran lefty Jim Deshaies goes 15–10, and Smith produces 25 saves. Davis's 34 homers and 89 RBIs top the offense. Soph catcher Craig Biggio hits 13 home runs.

1990

WE'VE GOT A REAL POWER FAILURE ON OUR HANDS!

Houston and Padres tie for fourth, and Astros' .242 average is lowest in NL. Veteran outfielder Franklin Stubbs leads team with 23 homers. Davis, limited by injuries and in final Houston season, hits 22. Righty Danny Darwin (11–4) leads NL with 2.21 ERA. Smith adds 23 saves.

Los Angeles Dodgers

1916 Rotund Wilbert Robinson, known to all as "Uncle Robbie," manages Dodgers to National League pennant by 2½ games over Philadelphia. Dodgers lose World Series to Boston Red Sox in five games.

1890 Brooklyn, which finished first in the American Association in 1889, is granted a National League franchise. It celebrates the occasion by winding up six games ahead of runner-up Chicago club.

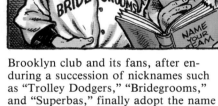

COACH, THIS ONE IS *REALLY* STUPID!

1906 Brooklyn club and its fans, after enduring a succession of nicknames such as "Trolley Dodgers," "Bridegrooms," and "Superbas," finally adopt the name "Dodgers."

MY VERY OWN FIELD OF DREAMS!

1913 Owner Charles H. Ebbets formally opens Ebbets Field. For the next 44 years it will be the scene of many memorable baseball events.

WE GOT SCALPED!

1920 Uncle Robbie and Dodgers rebound from three straight second-division finishes to win pennant from hated New York Giants by seven games. They lose five games to two vs. Cleveland in best-of-nine World Series.

1922 Right-handed speedballer Dazzy Vance, a 31-year-old "rookie," arrives in Brooklyn. He launches his Hall of Fame career when he wins the first of his seven straight strikeout titles.

MY BASE! NOPE. MY BASE! MY BASE!

1926 Dodgers' renowned slugger Babe Herman gains undying fame by hitting a two-base hit that leads to three Dodger runners being trapped at third base in August 15 game vs. Boston at Ebbets Field.

Larry MacPhail, known as "Loud Larry," becomes Dodgers' general manager and installs lights at Ebbets Field. On June 15, in first arclighter in Brooklyn, Cincinnati's Johnny Vander Meer no-hits Dodgers.

Leo (The Lip) Durocher, Dodgers' veteran shortstop, is named manager. Durocher launches controversial managerial career by leading Dodgers to third-place finish.

Right-handers Kirby Higbe and Whitlow Wyatt each win 22 games, and first baseman Dolf Camilli is NL's MVP. Brooklyn wins pennant, but catcher Mickey Owen's famed third-strike muff in Game 4 dooms Dodgers to five-game World Series defeat by Yankees.

Branch Rickey, longtime director of St. Louis Cardinals, becomes Dodgers' general manager. The cigar-smoking Rickey begins building a farm system that for the next decade makes Dodgers one of the game's most formidable ballclubs.

Branch Rickey breaks "color line" by introducing Jackie Robinson to majors. After Baseball Commissioner A. B. (Happy) Chandler bans Leo Durocher for the season, club's emergency manager, Burt Shotton, leads club to National League flag. Dodgers lose seven-game Series to Yankees, despite Cookie Lavagetto's ninth-inning, game-winning double that breaks up Bill Bevens's no-hitter in Game 4.

Dodgers lose National League flag to Philadelphia in season's final game. Walter O'Malley, in a series of front-office intrigues, ousts Branch Rickey and assumes presidency of club.

Jackie Robinson wins National League batting title (.342) and is named National League's MVP. Robinson leads Dodgers to pennant, but luckless ballclub fails again in World Series, bowing to Yankees in five games.

1963

Sandy Koufax wins 25 games and posts a 1.88 ERA. Dodgers win National League flag by six games over St. Louis. Then they amaze the baseball world by sweeping the Yankees four straight in the World Series.

1951

Manager Charlie Dressen, who has Dodgers leading National League by 13 games in mid-August, sees club lose best-of-three pennant playoff to rival Giants. Ralph Branca serves game-winning homer to Bobby Thomson in ninth inning of Game 3.

1953

ONE YEAR AT A TIME IS OK WITH ME!

Charlie Dressen rebounds from 1951 debacle to win NL flags in 1952 and 1953, but Dodgers bow to Yankees in both World Series. Dressen, seeking more than he is offered, gets dismissed by O'Malley, and relatively unknown Walter Alston becomes skipper.

1955

WHO'S A BUM NOW?!?

Lefty Johnny Podres pitches two wins in World Series. After five straight World Series losses to New York Yankees, Dodgers bring Brooklyn its only World Championship when Podres blanks Yankees, 2–0, in Game 7.

1957

Walter O'Malley finally makes the big move. Following Dodgers' slide to third place, he transfers the franchise from Brooklyn to Los Angeles, abandoning historic Ebbets Field and baseball's most rabid fans.

1959

After finishing woeful seventh in 1958, the club's first year in Los Angeles, the Dodgers make an amazing reversal. They not only win the National League flag in a two-game sweep of the Milwaukee Braves in a pennant playoff but also down the Chicago White Sox in a six-game World Series.

1962

WE WAS ROBBED!

...ER... YEAH!

Dodger Stadium becomes ballclub's brand-new home. Despite Don Drysdale's 25 wins and Maury Wills's record-setting 104 stolen bases, club loses pennant playoff to San Francisco Giants, two games to one.

Sandy Koufax wins 26 games and pitches fourth career no-hitter, a perfecto over Chicago Cubs on September 9. Dodgers win pennant over Giants by two games and down Minnesota in seven-game World Series. Koufax pitches shutouts in Games 5 and 7.

Sandy Koufax wins 27, with a 1.73 ERA. Bothered by an arthritic elbow, he announces his retirement following World Series, in which Baltimore knocks off Dodgers four in a row.

Tommy Lasorda's Dodgers defeat Cincinnati by 2½ games for West title, then beat Philadelphia for the pennant. But they again bow to Yankees in six-game World Series.

Rookie left-hander Fernando Valenzuela wins Cy Young Award in strike-marred season. Dodgers down Houston in Western Division playoff in five games and beat Montreal in five for National League pennant. After losing the first two, they upset Yankees in six-game World Series.

Dodgers win Western Division title by 5½ over Cincinnati. In best-of-seven National League pennant playoff they win the first two games, but drop four in a row to St. Louis.

Right-hander Orel Hershiser wins 23 — and National League's Cy Young Award by unanimous vote. Dodgers win West title over Cincinnati, then upset favored Mets in seven-game pennant playoff. Dodgers amaze baseball world by downing heavily favored Oakland A's in five-game World Series. Hershiser wins two games, and ailing Kirk Gibson hits game-winning pinch homer with two out in ninth inning of Game 1.

Coach Tommy Lasorda replaces future Hall of Famer Walter Alston, who managed Dodgers for 23 seasons. Dodgers respond by winning Western Division by 10 over Cincinnati and National League flag in best-of-five play-off vs. Philly. They lose World Series to Yankees in six games.

Montreal Expos

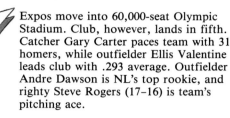

1977 Expos move into 60,000-seat Olympic Stadium. Club, however, lands in fifth. Catcher Gary Carter paces team with 31 homers, while outfielder Ellis Valentine leads club with .293 average. Outfielder Andre Dawson is NL's top rookie, and righty Steve Rogers (17–16) is team's pitching ace.

1969 Baseball goes international as Montreal joins National League. The expansion Expos lose 110 and finish last in six-team Eastern Division. Right fielder Rusty Staub is fan favorite with .302 average and 29 homers. Bill Stoneman is staff star at 11–19, plus no-hitter.

1979 Montreal wins club-record 95 games and finishes second in NL East. Third baseman Larry Parrish leads team with .307 average and 30 home runs. Dawson hits 25 and paces Expos with 92 RBIs. Lefty Bill Lee (16–10) is top pitcher.

1981 Expos win second half of strike-marred season. They defeat Phillies in playoff for NL East but are beaten by Dodgers in five-game pennant showdown. Dawson's 24 homers lead team. Tim Raines hits .304, and his 71 steals give him the first of his four straight stolen-base titles. Rogers (12–8) leads pitchers.

1985 Montreal lands in third for third time in last four seasons. Raines leads club with .320 average, while Dawson's 23 homers are one more than third baseman Tim Wallach delivers. Righty Bryn Smith is top pitcher with 18 wins. Relief ace Jeff Reardon sets club mark with 41 saves.

Montreal achieves third place, and Raines leads attack with .330 average. Wallach's 26 homers and 123 RBIs are best on club. Lefty Neal Heaton (13–10) tops staff, while righty Dennis Martinez goes 11–4 and Smith 10–9. Tim Burke becomes bullpen ace with 18 saves.

Another third-place windup, as first baseman Andres Galarraga leads squad with .302 average, 29 homers, and 92 RBIs. Martinez is the hill ace with 15 wins, while Smith and righty Pascual Perez and Jeff Parrett each win a dozen. Burke again posts 18 saves.

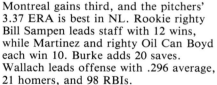

Expos go 81–81 and land fourth, with Galarraga leading them with 23 homers and 85 RBIs. Martinez tops moundsmen with 16 victories and lefty Mark Langston, in his lone Montreal season, goes 12–9. Burke is once again big man out of pen, winning nine and saving 28.

Montreal gains third, and the pitchers' 3.37 ERA is best in NL. Rookie righty Bill Sampen leads staff with 12 wins, while Martinez and righty Oil Can Boyd each win 10. Burke adds 20 saves. Wallach leads offense with .296 average, 21 homers, and 98 RBIs.

Expos fall to fourth, but Raines's .334 average nets him NL batting title. Dawson leads club with 20 homers and 78 RBIs. Righty Floyd Youmans (13–12) is staff's big winner, with Smith and righty Andy McGaffigan each winning 10. Reardon contributes 35 saves.

New York Mets

1969

The "miracle" year. Mets not only win newly minted Eastern Division but also upset Atlanta in NL flag playoff. They win World Series in five over favored Baltimore. Seaver's 25-7 earns him Cy Young Award, and Jones's .340 is club record.

IF MAN CAN LAND ON THE MOON... THE METS CAN WIN A WORLD SERIES!

THE 'OLD PERFESSER' IS BACK IN TOWN!

1962

The National League, after a four-year absence, returns to New York when expansion Mets are granted a franchise. The famed Casey Stengel, 71, manages the club. Mets lose 120 games but still match the successful Yankees in popularity.

MAYBE I—ED KRANEPOOL—CAN BE KNOWN AS THE "SHEA HEY" KID!

1964

Mets continue to occupy NL cellar, but do so in brand-new Shea Stadium, the site of Philly's Jim Bunning's perfect game in June and the All-Star Game in July. Bronx-born Ed Kranepool, 19, bats .257 in first full season, and Charley Smith leads club with 20 homers.

STENGEL

37

MUSTA TRIPPED OVER ONE OF THEM "ROAD APPLES"! —SEE YA, CASEY

1965

A broken hip compels Stengel to retire in August, and club again occupies cellar. Righty Jack Fisher (8-24) and lefty Al Jackson (8-20) are staff's top winners. Rookie outfielder Ron Swoboda paces team with 19 homers.

OUR HUNT FOR A SECOND BASEMAN IS OVER!

BOP!

1966

Manager Wes Westrum guides Mets to ninth with a 66-95 log. Righty Dennis Ribant (11-9) and right-handers Bob Shaw (11-10) and Jack Fisher (11-14) are mound "aces." Kranepool's 16 home runs lead squad, and second baseman Ron Hunt's .288 is best average.

TOM TERRIFIC!

1967

A return to NL cellar costs Westrum his job, but bright spot is right-hander Tom Seaver, who wins 16 and Rookie of the Year award. The USC product is only Met pitcher with winning record. Outfielder Tommy Davis, with 16 home runs and .302 average, paces Mets.

WHERE THERE'S A GIL, THERE'S A WAY!

1968

Gil Hodges named Mets' skipper and raises club to ninth place. Lefty Jerry Koosman (19-12) is rookie sensation, while Seaver goes 16-12. Third baseman Ed Charles's 15 homers top squad. Outfielder Cleon Jones hits .297, plus 14 homers.

Mets' third-place windup disappoints fans. Seaver wins 18 and Koosman 12, while lefty Tug McGraw (10 saves) and righty Ron Taylor (13 saves) lead the bullpen. Outfielder Tommie Agee hits 24 homers and first baseman Donn Clendenon hits 22 homers with 97 RBIs.

Another 83–79 season sinks Mets to fourth in NL East. Seaver (20–10) is NL's ERA leader at 1.76, and his career-high 289 strikeouts lead league. Nolan Ryan (10–14) is traded in December, a deal that still haunts the Mets.

Hodges's death, Yogi Berra's ascension to manager, and April deal for Rusty Staub highlight season in which Mets finish third. Seaver wins 21, and Jon Matlack's 15 earn him Rookie of the Year honors. John Milner hits 17 HRs, and Staub, despite injuries, bats .293.

Physical problems limit Seaver to 11–11 season, and Mets, lacking punch, sink to fifth, 20 games below .500. Milner's 20 homers lead squad, as do Staub's 78 RBIs. Koosman (15–11) and fellow lefty Matlack (13–15) are Berra's best hurlers.

Mets attain third, but Berra gets axed in late August. Seaver's 22 victories lead league, while Matlack goes 16–12 and Koosman 14–13. Righty-hitting Dave Kingman hits 36 home runs, while Staub, who is dealt to Detroit in December, drives in club-record 105 RBIs. Kranepool's .323 leads batting.

Minor-league skipper Joe Frazier manages Mets to another third-place windup, and Koosman is top pitcher with 21 wins. Seaver goes 14–11, and righty reliever Skip Lockwood saves 19. Kingman hits 37 homers, and Joe Torre, limited to 310 at-bats, hits .306.

Mets win another surprise pennant, taking Eastern Division in final weekend before upending Cincinnati in five-game flag playoff. Dream ends in seventh-game World Series loss to Oakland. Seaver (19–10) wins Cy Young. McGraw saves 25. Milner hits 23 homers, and Staub's 76 RBIs lead the club.

Torre replaces Frazier at helm in late May, and in mid-June Seaver and Kingman are traded. Mets lose 98 and crash into NL East cellar. Third baseman Lenny Randle leads regulars with .304 average. Nino Espinosa's 10 wins top staff. Lockwood saves 20.

Lefty first baseman Willie Montanez leads club in homers (17) and RBIs (96), as Mets again finish last. Switch-hitting center fielder Lee Mazzilli's .273 is club's best. Espinosa goes 11–15, while righty Pat Zachry is 10–6. Koosman's 3–15 earns him trade to Minnesota.

Bamberger quits in midseason, and Frank Howard manages Mets to another basement windup. Seaver returns and goes 9–14 (and is lost via draft following season). Lefty Jesse Orosco wins 13 and saves 17. Mets acquire Keith Hernandez in mid-June, and Darryl Strawberry hits 26 homers and earns NL Rookie of the Year prize.

Another basement windup occurs when righty Craig Swan's 14–13 is only .500-plus showing by Met pitchers. Righty-hitting outfielder Steve Henderson bats .306 and Mazzilli .303. Righty-hitting Joel Youngblood leads Mets in homers with 16.

Nelson Doubleday and Fred Wilpon buy Mets in January and watch club finish fifth with 67–95 record. Mazzilli's 16 homers lead squad, as do his 76 RBIs. Right-hander Mark Bomback's 10 wins are staff's best. Righty Neil Allen contributes 22 saves out of bullpen.

Another fifth-place finish in strike-shortened season costs Torre his job. Despite only 353 at-bats, Kingman returns to lead club with 22 homers and 59 RBIs. Staub also returns and bats .317. Allen is again mound's bright spot, going 7–6 with 18 saves.

George Bamberger skippers club to 65–97 record and residence in NL East basement. Kingman's 37 homers lead National League, but he bats only .204. Righty-hitting outfielder George Foster hits 13 homers, and catcher John Stearns leads Mets with .293 average. Swan's 11 wins pace moundsmen.

Davey Johnson becomes manager and hikes club to second, as rookie Dwight Gooden wins 17, sets NL freshman mark for Ks (276), and is Rookie of the Year. Darling wins 12, Orosco saves 31. Hernandez leads club with .311 average. Strawberry hits 26 HRs and has 97 RBIs.

Mets go 108–54. They defeat Houston for NL flag and Boston in World Series. Ojeda leads with 18 wins, one more than Gooden. McDowell (22 saves) and Orosco (21 saves) lead the bullpen. Strawberry's 27 homers pace Mets, as do Carter's 105 RBIs.

Despite 92 wins, Mets must settle for second in NL East. Gooden, idled until June because of rehabilitation, goes 15–7, and McDowell leads pen with 25 saves. Strawberry hits 39 homers, while third baseman Howard Johnson socks 36.

Mets win 100 and NL East by 15 games but are upended by Dodgers in seven-game pennant playoff. Soph right-hander David Cone goes 20–3, and Gooden is 18–9. Darling wins 17, while lefty reliever Randy Myers saves 26. Strawberry's 39 homers lead NL.

Mets finish second, six games behind Cubs, as Johnson leads club with 36 homers and 101 RBIs. Strawberry hits 29 homers and outfielder Kevin McReynolds 22. Myers saves 24, while Cone, Darling, and lefty Sid Fernandez each win 14. Gooden (9–4) is idled two months by shoulder ailment.

It's another second-place finish, as Bud Harrelson replaces Davey Johnson at helm in May. Lefty Frank Viola wins 20 and Gooden 19. Lefty reliever John Franco saves 33. Strawberry, who goes to Los Angeles as free agent in November, hits 37 homers, while first baseman Dave Magadan bats .328.

Mets win 98 but finish second, three games behind St. Louis. Gooden's 24 wins and 1.53 ERA both lead NL, and he's Cy Young winner. Darling goes 16–6, while Orosco and reliever Roger McDowell each save 17. Catcher Gary Carter, obtained from Montreal, paces club with 32 home runs and 100 RBIs.

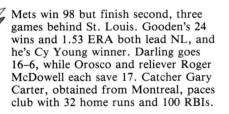

Philadelphia Phillies

1915 The Phillies with their first pennant, under freshman manager Pat Moran. Right-handed Hall of Famer Grover Cleveland Alexander wins 31 and leads NL with 241 strikeouts. Outfielder Cliff Cravath paces NL with 24 homers and 115 RBIs. Phillies, however, lose World Series to Boston in five games.

The first game in National League history is played on April 22 in Philadelphia, with Boston winning, 6–5. Late in the season, with a 14–45 record, the Philadelphia club disbands, and the NL reclaims the franchise.

Philadelphia is readmitted to the National League when the Worcester franchise is transferred. The club, known as the Quakers, finishes last in the eight-club league. First baseman Sid Farrar becomes more famous as the father of opera star Geraldine Farrar.

Despite .315 club batting average, Phillies' dearth of pitching lock them in NL cellar with 102 defeats. Outfielder Chuck Klein hits .386 and slams 40 homers, but the staff's 6.71 ERA dooms his efforts. Phil Collins (16–11) is only pitcher with winning record.

After 51 years at antiquated Baker Bowl, Phillies move to Shibe Park as tenants of the AL A's on July 4. The change has no real effect, as the Phillies finish last with 105 losses and begin a five-year residency in the National League cellar.

After five straight cellar finishes, the Phillies rise to seventh place. In November the financially secure Carpenter clan begins its 38-year ownership of the franchise. Though improvement is slow at first, one of the moves—to rename the club the "Blue Jays"—fails with the fans and the media.

Following 16 seasons of second-division baseball—eight of them cellar windups—Philadelphia, under new manager Eddie Sawyer, lands in third place. Outfielder Del Ennis, 25 homers and 110 RBIs, leads the club. Lefty Ken Heintzelman and righty Russ Meyer each win 17.

Roberts goes 28–7, and lefty Curt Simmons, a former $65,000 bonus signee, wins 14, but Philly finishes fourth. Ennis with 20 homers and 107 RBIs again paces the club offensively.

Gene Mauch, in his first full season as manager, suffers a record 23 straight defeats in July and August, as the club lands in the cellar for the fourth straight year, losing 107 games. Art Mahaffey (11–19) is top winner. No other starter wins more than six games.

The NL expands to 10 clubs, and the Phillies land in seventh, with an 81–80 record, their first .500-plus season in a decade. Mahaffey goes 19–14 to pace the pitchers. Don Demeter leads regulars with batting average of .307, plus 29 home runs and 107 RBIs.

Despite 92 wins, the Phillies tie with Cincinnati for second. Jim Bunning wins 19, including a perfect game over the Mets, while outfielder Johnny Callison hits 31 homers and has 104 RBIs. Richie Allen hits .318, with 29 homers, and is NL Rookie of the Year.

The Phillies move into brand-new Veterans Stadium on April 10 and ice that cake with a 4–1 win over Montreal. Philly finishes sixth in the six-club NL East, with Deron Johnson hitting 34 homers. Righty Rick Wise (17–14) and lefty Woodie Fryman (10–7) supply the pitching.

A spring-training swap brings lefty Steve Carlton from St. Louis, and he wins 27 of the club's 59 victories and the Cy Young Award. No other Philly pitcher is above .500. Greg Luzinski leads the club with 18 homers.

Right-hander Robin Roberts ends the Phillies' 35-year flag drought when he wins No. 20 on Dick Sisler's three-run homer at Brooklyn on the final day of the season. Reliever Jim Konstanty wins 16 and is the NL's MVP. Philly, however, is erased in four straight by Yankees in World Series.

1977

Carlton's 23 wins and Cy Young prize spearhead club's second straight Eastern title. Right-hander Larry Christenson wins career-high 19, and Garber has 19 saves. Luzinski, batting .309, paces club with 39 homers, one more than Schmidt. Phillies are downed in pennant playoff, by Los Angeles.

1973

OZARK, WE'VE GOT A REAL MOUNTAIN TO CLIMB!

Philly, with Danny Ozark as skipper, occupies the basement for the third straight year, and Carlton, despite leading the NL with 293 innings, goes 13–20. Luzinski is Mr. Power, with 29 homers. Mike Schmidt, despite a .196 average, hits 18 homers.

1974

3RD Place

WE'RE GETTIN' THERE!

Righty Jim Lonborg wins 17 and Carlton 16, as Phillies jump to third in NL East. First baseman Willie Montanez leads club with .304 average, and Schmidt's 36 home runs pace NL. His 116 RBIs are the most by a Phillies' batter in 19 years.

1975

POW!

The Phillies edge into second, their best finish in 11 years. Schmidt, with 38, leads NL in homers, while Luzinski bops 34 and paces NL with 120 RBIs. Carlton (15–14) is club's top winner, while righty reliever Gene Garber and lefty Tug McGraw each have 14 saves.

1976

...YES OFFICER, IT WAS A BIG RED MACHINE!

A club-record 101 victories give Philly NL East title. Carlton goes 20–7 and Lonborg 18–10. Righty Ron Reed leads with 14 saves, and Schmidt's 38 home runs again pace league. Luzinski hits .304 with 21 homers, but season is stained by Cincinnati's sweep in best-of-five pennant playoff.

1978

WHACK! 35

Ozark's third straight divisional title is certified by Carlton's 16 wins, plus Luzinski's 35 homers and 101 RBIs. Schmidt hits 21 homers. Reed, with 17 saves, and McGraw, with nine, head Philly bullpen. Dodgers again mar Phillies' year by winning pennant play-off, three games to one.

1980

WE'RE ALL PHILLY PHANATICS!

Phillies, under Dallas Green, finally win it all. They beat Montreal for East crown, edge Houston for NL flag, and capture first World Series with six-game win over Kansas City. Carlton (24–9) wins Cy Young Award, and Schmidt's league-leading 48 home runs earn him MVP.

1982 ...ANOTHER ONE FOR MY COLLECTION!

Carlton's 23–11 season earns him fourth Cy Young, but Phillies, under Pat Corrales, finish second. Schmidt, with 35 homers and 87 RBIs leads attack. He is aided by Gary Matthews, with 19 homers and 83 RBIs. Catcher Bo Diaz hits 18 homers and drives in 85.

1983 WE SALUTE THE FLAG! N.L. CHAMPS

Corrales is replaced by general manager Paul Owens. Move results in divisional title and NL pennant win over Dodgers. But Baltimore wins World Series in five. John Denny (19–6) wins Cy Young, and Schmidt's 40 homers give him NL lead. Reliever Al Holland has 25 saves.

1986 Despite finishing second to Mets by 21½ lengths, Schmidt wins third MVP award. His 37 homers give him eighth homer title, an NL record. Pitching is a problem, as Kevin Gross (12–12) is club's biggest winner. Righty reliever Steve Bedrosian does chip in with 29 saves.

1987 LEAVE IT TO STEVE!

The Phillies slide to fourth-place tie with Pittsburgh. Lefty Shane Rawley (17–11) paces the staff, and Bedrosian contributes 40 saves. Schmidt, as he has done so often, leads the powermen with 35 homers and 113 RBIs.

1988 COME IN, LEE...

Lee Elia is axed as manager, and Phillies settle into NL East dungeon with 96 defeats. The club doesn't have a regular pitcher who wins more games than he loses, and Gross is tops in victories with 12. Bedrosian saves 28, and James leads club with 19 homers.

1989 SEE YA'! EXIT SCHMIDT 20

Schmidt terminates his career by retiring in late May, and Phillies, under rookie skipper Nick Leyva, land in the NL East cellar with 67–95 record. Lefty-hitting outfielder Von Hayes provides the offense, with 26 homers and 78 RBIs.

1990 "NAILS" RARELY FAILS! .325

The Phillies improve to fourth-place tie with Chicago. Outfielder Len Dykstra's .325 average leads the club. Hayes again paces club with 17 homers and 73 RBIs. Outfielder Dale Murphy, obtained from Atlanta late in season, hits seven homers in 57 games.

Pittsburgh Pirates

1901

Manager Fred Clarke, with Hall of Famer Honus Wagner his biggest star, leads Pittsburgh to first of three straight National League flags. Clarke and Wagner were teammates at Louisville, and when that franchise was moved to Pittsburgh in 1900, the pair came along.

I'M WITH YOU, BUDDY!

1887

WHAT CAN I SAY? THE ALLEGHENIES HAVE MADE NO GAINS!

The Pittsburgh franchise, known as the Alleghenies, debuts in the National League, finishing sixth. The club's annual output until the advent of the 20th century is almost always a second-division effort.

1891

...THEY MADE HIM AN OFFER HE COULDN'T REFUSE!

Pittsburgh gains its famed name of "Pirates" when, following the folding of the Players' League in 1890, second baseman Louis Bierbauer stays with Pittsburgh rather than report to club he was assigned to as per the "peace treaty."

1903

WE DARE YA'!

Pirates win NL flag and challenge AL Boston club to what is to become the annual World Series. Boston wins in upset. Wagner, who will win eight NL batting titles, leads league with .355, while Sam Leever (25) and Deacon Phillippe (24) lead staff in wins.

1909

THE FINISHING TOUCH!

Pirates move into brand-new Forbes Field and win the pennant. Howard Camnitz (25) and Vic Willis (22) are club's pitching leaders. With rookie right-hander Babe Adams winning three games, they best Detroit in seven-game World Series.

1925

WHAT A LUXURY!

With seven .300 hitters in his starting lineup, manager Bill McKechnie leads Bucs to first flag since 1909. Kiki Cuyler leads Pittsburgh with .357 average, and right-hander Lee Meadows paces staff with 19 wins. In World Series they rebound from 1–3 deficit to win title from Washington.

1927

Lefty-hitting Paul Waner takes National League batting crown with .380, and right-hander Carmen Hill wins 22. Manager Donie Bush wins National League flag, but in World Series, Buccos are swept four straight by mighty New York Yankees.

Despite a seven-game lead on September 1, manager Pie Traynor's Pirates' lack of pitching stalls them in final month, and they finish second to Chicago. Arky Vaughan leads club with .322 average. Paul Waner's younger brother, Lloyd, also a Hall of Famer, hits .313.

Outfielder Ralph Kiner, who led NL in 1946 with 23 homers and who will wear NL homer crown through 1952, hits 51 to tie Johnny Mize for league lead. Despite Kiner's power, Pirates land in cellar, with lefty Fritz Ostermueller (12) their top winner.

On May 26, at Milwaukee, Harvey Haddix pitches one of the greatest games in history. The lefty retires 36 straight batters before an error and Hank Aaron's base hit defeat him, 1–0. It's the first and only time a perfect pitching performance is carried beyond nine innings.

After 33-year pennant drought, Pirates, under Danny Murtaugh, win National League pennant. They upset favored Yankees in seven-game World Series, which Bill Mazeroski wins with ninth-inning homer—the only time a Series has ended on a four-base blast.

Pirates move into brand-new Three Rivers Stadium, and Murtaugh, in the third of his four tours as Bucs' manager, leads team to National League East flag. Lefty Luke Walker (15) is staff's top winner, and outfielder Roberto Clemente's .352 paces Pittsburgh's batsmen.

Pittsburgh upsets Baltimore in seven-game World Series, as righthander Steve Blass, 15–8 during the season, wins two Series games. Clemente's .341 leads club, and outfielder Willie Stargell's 48 homers top National League. Right-hander Dock Ellis wins 19.

Bill Virdon manages club to third straight Eastern title but loses five-game flag playoff to Cincinnati. Clemente collects 3000th career hit in September and then perishes in New Year's Eve plane crash while flying supplies to earthquake victims in Nicaragua.

1979

"POPS" IS TOPS!

Chuck Tanner, following two second-place windups, manages Bucs to National League pennant. He then sees his squad upset Baltimore in seven-game series after trailing 3-1 in games. Candelaria, with 14, is Bucs' top winner, and righty reliever Kent Tekulve contributes 31 saves. Stargell, at 39, hits 32 homers and shares the National League MVP award.

In special election, Clemente is voted into Hall of Fame in March. Virdon is replaced by Murtaugh as skipper in September. Bucs slide to third place despite Stargell's league-leading 44 homers. Pitching is biggest problem, as Nelson Briles (14) is club leader.

THIS WAY, BUCKOS!

Murtaugh guides club to East crown, but Dodgers take National League flag in best-of-five playoff. Stargell's 25 homers lead Pirates, and lefty-hitting Al Oliver's .321 tops club at plate. Left-hander Jerry Reuss paces staff with 16 victories.

THE PLAYOFFS WERE A BIG RED SWEEP!

Murtaugh again leads Pirates to East title, but Cincinnati wins playoff for flag in three-game sweep. Reuss, with 18 victories, leads Pittsburgh pitchers, while outfielder Dave Parker paces club with 25 home runs.

The Pirates finish second to Phillies, and Murtaugh, who resigns following season, passes away in December at age 59. Lefty John Candelaria is Bucs' top winner with 16, while Oliver's .323 leads Pirates at the plate.

DOES ANYONE HAVE ANY QUALITY PITCHING IN THEM TODAY?

BULLPEN

A lack of quality pitching—Don Robinson's 15 wins top the staff—prevents Pittsburgh from finishing better than fourth in National League East. Lefty-hitting first baseman Jason Thompson leads club with 31 homers and 101 RBIs.

Tanner guides Pirates to second place, getting 15 victories from Candelaria and 15 from lefty Larry McWilliams and 18 saves from bullpen ace Tekulve. Righty-hitting infielder Bill Madlock bats .323 to lead the National League.

Pirates' bats turn cold, and pitching, always somewhat spotty, dooms club to basement windup in NL East race. Right-hander Rick Rhoden (14–9) is top winner, and Tekulve, in his final season with Bucs, saves 13, while Madlock's batting average drops 70 points.

Another cellar finish, this one with 104 defeats, costs Tanner his managerial post. Righty Rick Reuschel (14–8) is the only starter with a winning record. Thompson, in his final season in Pittsburgh, leads squad with a dozen home runs.

Jim Leyland, a minor-league manager, is named Pirates' skipper but is unable to transfer club from National League basement. Rhoden (15–12) is his best pitcher, and switch-hitting second baseman Johnny Ray bats .301 to pace Pirates' hitters.

A series of trades, one of which brings outfielder Andy Van Slyke and lefty-hitting catcher Mike LaValliere from St. Louis, helps raise Bucs to fifth place. Right-handed newcomer Mike Dunne (13–6) leads pitchers, while sophomore outfielder Barry Bonds paces team with 25 homers.

The Pirates are outdistanced by division-winning Mets by 15 games, but Bucs' second-place finish is well received in Pittsburgh. Van Slyke leads club with 25 homers, one more than Bonds and switch-hitting Bobby Bonilla.

Injuries to key players drop Pirates to fifth. Doug Drabek (14–12) is top pitcher, and righty reliever Bill Landrum chalks up 26 saves. Bonilla's 24 homers supply power, while LaValliere leads squad with .316 average.

Drabek's 22–6 record earns him Cy Young Award, and Bonds' .301 average and 33 homers, 52 stolen bases, and 114 RBIs get him MVP prize. Bucs capture National League East, but their season ends on sour note when Cincinnati defeats them in best-of-seven playoff for the National League flag.

St. Louis Cardinals

1924

Hornsby assures his future Hall of Fame ranking when he bats .424—the highest major-league average in the 20th century.

1876

WOW! A NO-HITTER! I BET NO ONE EVER DOES *THAT* AGAIN!

St. Louis becomes charter member of the National League. Pitcher George Washington Bradley wins 45 games, including league-leading 16 shutouts, and tosses National League's first no-hitter, July 15 vs. Hartford.

1899

BOYS, WE HAVE NICE UNIFORMS, BUT THIS TEAM IS FOR THE BIRDS!

Despite succession of second-division finishes, St. Louis' red-trimmed uniforms earn them what is to become one of baseball's more colorful names: "Cardinals."

1920

BOP!

.370! I GUESS IT'S JUST AN OFF-YEAR!

Rogers Hornsby wins the first of his National League record of six straight batting titles. He hits .370, although Redbirds finish in sixth place.

1926

IT'S THE YANKEES CRYIN' 'FOWL' NOW!

In 1925 Hornsby replaced Branch Rickey as manager so Rickey could devote his time to extending a farm system that would become famous. In 1926 Hornsby leads Cardinals to their first flag and a seven-game upset of New York Yankees in World Series.

1931

THIS PEPPER IS THE SPICE IN THE LINEUP!

Hall of Fame outfielder Chick Hafey leads National League with .349 batting average. Outfielder Pepper Martin's batting and baserunning feats lead Redbirds to pennant by 13 games over New York Giants and seven-game World Series win over Philadelphia A's.

1934

OH NO!

IT'S THE 'DEAN' MACHINE!

Right-hander Dizzy Dean wins 30 games, and younger brother Paul wins 19. Cardinals clinch National League flag on final weekend of season from New York Giants. Brothers then win two games apiece in seven-game World Series triumph over Detroit Tigers.

Hall of Fame outfielder Joe (Ducky) Medwick's .374 batting average leads National League. His 31 homers and 154 RBIs make him the last National Leaguer to win hitting's Triple Crown.

Hall of Fame first baseman Johnny Mize's 43 homers tops the National League. This remains Birds' one-season homer mark to this day.

Right-hander Mort Cooper wins 22 games, and Cardinals win club record of 106. They take National League flag over runner-up Brooklyn Dodgers, and then go on to upset favored New York Yankees in a five-game World Series.

Shortstop Marty Marion is the National League's Most Valuable Player. Redbirds win their third straight pennant and defeat crosstown rival St. Louis Browns in six-game World Series.

Cardinals win flag by defeating Brooklyn in best-of-three pennant play-off and upset Boston Red Sox in seven-game World Series. Left-hander Harry Brecheen wins three in Series, and Birds triumph on Enos Slaughter's winning run slide in final game at St. Louis.

Musial, pinch-hitting in the sixth inning of a game at Chicago, bangs a double off the Cubs' Moe Drabowsky for his 3,000th career base hit in a 5–3 Redbirds' victory.

Hall of Famer Stan Musial bats career-high .376 and wins his third MVP award and the third of his seven National League batting titles. He leads National League in hits (230), doubles (46), triples (18), and RBIs (131).

1968

Despite Gibson's 22 wins and record 1.12 ERA during pennant-winning season, the Cardinals, leading three games to one, are upset by Detroit Tigers in seven-game World Series.

1963

Musial, at age 42, retires as an active player and moves into Cardinals' front office, after finishing career with .331 batting average.

1964

HEY GIBBY! SAVE SOME FOR US!

Hall of Fame right-hander Bob Gibson wins 19 games. Cardinals end 17-year pennant drought with victory on season's final day. Gibby wins two more in seven-game World Series win over New York Yankees.

1967

HEY! BIRDWATCHING CAN BE FUN!

Manager Red Schoendienst watches his Redbirds win 101 regular-season games and National League flag. Gibson wins three complete games in seven-game WorldSeries win over the Boston Red Sox. Hall of Fame outfielder Lou Brock steals record seven bases in Series.

1969

19 K'S AND I STILL LOSE! I THINK IT'S GONNA BE A METS' YEAR...

Left-hander Steve Carlton, who is later to become a 300-game winner, strikes out then-record 19 New York Mets in September 15 game — which he loses, 4–3. Earlier in season, Stan Musial is formally admitted to the Hall of Fame.

1971

TORRE'S GLORY!

Joe Torre pushes Cardinals to second-place finish in National League East with a league-leading .363 batting average, which also earns him the National League's Most Valuable Player prize.

1972

WE DID OUR USUAL BEST!

Bob Gibson strikes out 200 or more batters for then-record ninth time. Lou Brock extends his record of stealing 50 or more bases in consecutive seasons to eight, despite Birds' fourth-place finish.

Brock steals one-season record of 118 bases. Gibson becomes only the second right-hander in history to fan 3,000 batters in a career.

Whitey Herzog, who became Cardinals' manager in 1980, leads Birds to NL flag with three straight wins over Atlanta in NL Championship Series. He then guides club from three-games-to-two deficit in World Series to seven-game victory over Milwaukee.

Rookie outfielder Vince Coleman sets freshman mark for stealing bases in season with 110. Birds down Los Angeles Dodgers for NL pennant but lose seven-game World Series to Kansas City Royals. Earlier in season, Lou Brock is elected to Hall of Fame.

Whitey Herzog again leads his Redbirds to National League East title and National League flag. They defeat San Francisco Giants in seven-game playoff after trailing 3–2. In World Series against the Minnesota Twins, the Birds are beaten in seventh game of a Series that sets a record when the home team wins every game.

Despite succession of injuries to key personnel, Herzog keeps Cardinals in National League East chase until final week. Veteran shortstop Ozzie Smith continues to dazzle defensively, winning his eighth consecutive Gold Glove Award.

Herzog, who managed Birds to three flags in 1980s, resigns in midseason. Shortly after, Joe Torre, one of Cardinals' most popular players during his active days, signs long-term contract as Herzog's replacement.

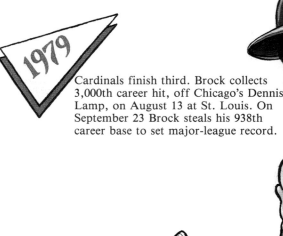

Cardinals finish third. Brock collects 3,000th career hit, off Chicago's Dennis Lamp, on August 13 at St. Louis. On September 23 Brock steals his 938th career base to set major-league record.

San Diego Padres

 **1976**

Jones leads NL with 22 victoruies, and righty reliever Butch Metzger goes 11–4 with 16 saves. Winfield's 13 homers top Padres, while first baseman Mike Ivie leads squad with .291 average and 70 RBIs. San Diego's 73–89 record lands them fifth in NL West.

... AND THEN ALONG CAME JONES!

1969

PADRES, SAY YOUR PRAYERS!

National League expands to 12 clubs, with the San Diego Padres joining the newly minted Western Division. Padres, as expected, finish last, losing a club-record 110 games. First baseman Nate Colbert leads team with 24 homers and 66 RBIs.

1974

WELL, IT'S PROBABLY BETTER THAN MOVING TO D.C.!

Hamburger king Ray Kroc, of McDonald's fame, rescues club from possible transfer to Washington, D.C., when he buys Padres. Despite 22 homers by Willie McCovey and 20 from Dave Winfield, club finishes in cellar for sixth straight year.

1975

...AND WILLIE SOCKS ANOTHER ONE!

Padres finally desert basement and finish fourth, as lefty Randy Jones goes 20–12 and his 2.24 ERA is NL's tops. McCovey, with 23, and Winfield, with 15, provide home-run sock. Other than Jones, no other Padre hurler pitches better than .500.

1977

IT'S ALWAYS DARKEST BEFORE THE DAWN!

Another fifth-place windup, as Alvin Dark replaces John McNamara as manager. Lefty Bob Shirley (12–18) is club's big winner. Outfielder George Hendrick leads team with .311 average, and Winfield's 25 homers and 92 RBIs provide biggest punch.

San Diego finally breaks even (81–81) and finishes fourth under skipper Dick Williams. Lefty Tim Lollar wins career-high 16, while righty John Montefusco and Eric Show each win 10. Catcher Terry Kennedy leads team with .295 average, 21 homers, and 97 RBIs.

It's another 81–81 windup in fourth, as Kennedy paces squad with 17 homers and 98 RBIs. Free agent Steve Garvey bats .294 with 14 home runs. Show's 15–12 log is best on staff, while lefty Dave Dravecky goes 14–10.

Padres win NL West by 12 lengths and upend Cubs in flag playoff before bowing to Detroit in World Series. Tony Gwynn's .351 average wins NL batting crown, while Graig Nettles and Kevin McReynolds each hit 20 homers. Show (15–9) is top pitcher, while reliever Goose Gossage saves 25.

San Diego finishes third, tied with Houston. Gwynn bats .317, and outfielder Carmelo Martinez cracks 21 homers. Righty Andy Hawkins is tops with 18 wins, while righty LaMarr Hoyt goes 16–8. Gossage produces 26 saves.

Manager Roger Craig guides Padres to fourth place with 84–78 mark. Veteran righty Gaylord Perry (21–6) tops NL in wins. Reliever Rollie Fingers produces 37 saves. Outfielder Gene Richards and Winfield lead hitters with .308 average, while latter's 24 homers and 97 RBIs produce the power.

1989

Padres finish second, and Gwynn wins third straight batting title with .336 average. Free agent Jack Clark hits 26 homers and has 94 RBIs. Whitson (16–11) and lefty Bruce Hurst (15–11) are staff's best. Davis's 44 saves earn him Cy Young Award.

1986

THERE GOES ANOTHER McHOMER!

POW!

Padres slip to fourth in NL West despite Gwynn's .329 average, plus 26 homers and 96 RBIs from McReynolds. Hawkins and righty Lance McCullers head staff with 10 wins each. Gossage remains bullpen ace with 21 saves.

1987

BENITO TURNED OUT TO BE QUITE A CATCH!

San Diego falls into last place. Gwynn wins second NL title with .370 average. Soph first baseman John Kruk bats .313 with 20 homers. Catcher Benito Santiago, NL's Rookie of the Year, hits .300. Ed Whitson (10–13) is biggest winner, while McCullers registers 16 saves.

1988

I'LL SHOW 'EM!

Padres rebound to third place, as Gwynn's .313 nets him NL batting crown. Martinez paces attack with 18 homers. Show's 16 wins top staff. Hawkins and lefty Dennis Rasmussen each win 14. Southpaw Mark Davis, with 28 saves, is bullpen star.

1990

"BIP" BOP!

.309

The Padres tie Houston for fourth. Gwynn and switch-hitting Bip Roberts lead club with .309 averages, while Clark's 25 homers top roster. Outfielder Joe Carter hits 24 and drives in 115 runs. Whitson (14–9) is again the mound leader.

San Francisco Giants

McGraw, with immortal Christy Mathewson winning 31, leads Giants to second straight NL flag. Matty's fellow righties include Red Ames (22–8) and Iron Man McGinnity (21–15). Matty wins a record three shutouts in the World Series win over the A's.

The National League shifts its ailing Troy, N.Y. franchise into the big city, and two years later manager Jim Mutrie inadvertently gives his club a nickname when he describes them as "My big fellows! My giants." By turn of the century, team is among also-rans.

Doomed to the NL cellar, the Giants make momentous decision when they sign John McGraw as manager. He will lead the team for next 30 years, winning 10 pennants and three World Championships, and will become one of the most famous managers in history.

Giants finish second when they drop postseason playoff game to Cubs. The game is necessitated by the Sept. 23 match between the two teams ending in 1–1 tie when Giants' Fred Merkle fails to touch second, thus nullifying Giants' win.

Mathewson wins 26, and lefty Rube Marquard 24, as Giants win flag by 7½ over Chicago. Catcher Chief Meyers leads Giants with .332 average, while second baseman Larry Doyle hits .310 and leads club with 13 homers. But Giants lose six-game World Series to Connie Mack's A's.

Giants win NL flag by 11 over Cubs but are defeated by Red Sox in World Series when outfielder Fred Snodgrass drops fly enabling Boston to rally to win final game. Marquard, who wins record 19 in a row during season, chalks up 26 victories and Mathewson 23.

A third straight NL pennant, won by 12½ over Phillies, is spoiled by another World Series loss, this one to A's. Mathewson (25–11), Marquard (23–10), and righty Jeff Tesreau (22–13) lead McGraw's squad.

McGraw's rebuilding pays off in another pennant, but also another Series defeat, by the White Sox. Lefty Ferdie Schupp (21–7) leads the staff, while Benny Kauff (.308) and George Burns (.302) pace the attack. Davy Robertson leads NL with 12 home runs.

Giants win first of four straight flags and then defeat the Yankees in World Series. Lefty Art Nehf (20–10) is club's mound ace, and third baseman Frankie Frisch bats .341. First baseman George Kelly (.308) leads NL with 23 homers.

Another Series win, this one in four straight over Yankees, though Game 2 ends in tie. Outfielder Casey Stengel hits .368, and Ross Youngs and left fielder Irish Meusel each bat .331.

Giants have fine season in NL but are upset by Yankees in World Series. Frisch, a second baseman now, leads squad with .348 average, while Stengel, a part-timer, hits .339, plus two homers in Series, one an inside-the-park drive at Yankee Stadium.

After winning pennant over Brooklyn by 1½ games, Giants lose seven-game Series to Washington. Giants lead NL with .300 average. Youngs paces club with .356, while Frisch (.328), Kelly (.324), and Meusel (.310) make it easier for staff, headed by righty Virgil Barnes (16–10) and lefty Jack Bentley (16–5).

In June, with club in second division, McGraw resigns as manager, and Bill Terry replaces him. In eight years since last flag, Giants have introduced such Hall of Famers as Mel Ott and Carl Hubbell, Freddie Fitzsimmons, plus future Polo Grounds favorites Jo-Jo Moore and Hal Schumacher.

Terry leads Giants to flag, plus World Series triumph over Washington. Hubbell's 23 victories lead NL. Schumacher wins 19. Terry paces club with .322 average, and Ott hammers 23 homers and accounts for 103 RBIs.

SAY HEY!

1954

Mays returns from military and is NL's MVP on league-leading .345 average, plus 41 homers and 110 RBIs. Giants pull four-straight Series upset over favored Cleveland, as Mays makes famed catch in Game 1 and pinch hitter Dusty Rhodes helps eliminate Indians.

1936

CARL'S OUR "MEAL TICKET"!

Giants win pennant but are defeated by Yankees in six-game World Series. Hubbell's 26 wins and 2.31 ERA lead NL. Ott bats .328 and paces NL with 33 home runs. Moore bats .316, while Terry, in final season, hits .310.

1937

BOYS, IT'S ANOTHER "SUBWAY SERIES," SO WE'RE GIVING YOU ALL FREE TOKENS!

Hubbell leads NL with 22 wins, while rookie lefty Cliff Melton goes 20–9. Despite five-game World Series loss to Yankees, some Giants enjoy banner season. Ott's 31 homers lead NL, while outfielder Jimmy Ripple hits .317 and Moore .310.

1942

...AND I DON'T WANT TO HEAR ANYONE SAY I "OTT" TO HAVE DONE BETTER!

Giants, with Ott in first year as manager, end three years of second-division finishes by landing in third place. Ott again leads league in homers (30), while Mize hits 26 and leads NL in RBIs with 110. Pitching, however, is only so-so, with Lohrman (13–4) the club ace.

1948

JUST CALL ME "LEO THE LIP"!

Ott resigns in July, and baseball world is stunned when longtime Dodger Leo Durocher replaces him. Durocher begins rebuilding second-division Giants, and his efforts begin to pay future dividends.

1951

THE GIANTS WIN THE PENNANT! THE GIANTS WIN THE PENNANT!

POW!

Rookie wonder Willie Mays arrives in late May, and his inspiring play fuels comeback from 13½-game deficit in mid-August to pennant, via playoff and Bobby Thomson's homer, over Dodgers. Righties Sal Maglie and Larry Jansen each win 23, but club loses six-game World Series to Yankees.

1958

CALIFORNIA, HERE WE COME!

GIANTS BASEBALL CLUB

In a stunning move, Giants join Dodgers in California, moving to San Francisco. Mays' .347 and 29 homers lead club, while first baseman Orlando Cepeda bats .312 with 25 homers and becomes NL's Rookie of the Year. Giants land in third.

Giants defeat Dodgers in flag playoff but lose World Series to Yankees in seven games. Mays leads NL with 49 homers and club with 141 RBIs. Jack Sanford leads staff with 24 wins. Felipe Alou leads club with .316 average, while Cepeda hits .306, plus 35 homers.

Giants finish second in NL West, as MVP and future Hall of Famer Willie McCovey bats .320 and leads NL with 45 homers and 126 RBIs. Juan Marichal wins 21, and his 2.10 ERA paces NL hurlers.

Giants take NL West title but lose to Pittsburgh in pennant playoff. Marichal (18–11) and Gaylord Perry (16–12) lead the moundsmen, and outfielder Bobby Bonds paces Giants with 33 homers and 102 RBIs. Mays, at 40, plays his final Giant season and hits 18 home runs.

Roger Craig manages Giants to Western Division title, but club loses flag playoff to Cardinals. Soph first baseman Will Clark leads regulars with .308 average, 35 homers, and 91 RBIs. Third baseman Kevin Mitchell, obtained from San Diego in July, bats .306. Mike LaCoss (13–10) is top pitcher.

Giants slide to fourth, but Clark leads NL with 109 RBIs. He also paces team with 29 homers, while Mitchell hits 19. Right-hander Rick Reuschel paces pitchers with 19 victories, and righty Kelly Downs goes 13–9. Righty Scott Garrelts heads pen with 13 saves.

Giants land third in NL West, as Mitchell leads club with 35 homers and third baseman Matt Williams paces NL with 122 RBIs. Center fielder Brett Butler leads club with .309 average and 51 stolen bases. Rookie righty John Burkett heads staff with 14 wins, and righty reliever Steve Bedrosian contributes 17 saves.

Craig leads Giants to divisional crown plus pennant, via playoff win over Cubs. However, Giants bow in four straight to Oakland in earthquake-plagued World Series. Mitchell, NL's MVP, leads league with 47 homers and 125 RBIs, while Clark's .333 leads club in average. Reuschel, 17–8, is top hurler.